Green Line 2

Vorschläge zur Leistungsmessung

von
Pauline Ashworth
Elise Köhler-Davidson
Carolyn Jones
Stefan Rauschenberg

herausgegeben von
Harald Weisshaar

Ernst Klett Verlag
Stuttgart · Leipzig

Vorwort

Liebe Lehrerin, lieber Lehrer,

die *Green Line 2 Vorschläge zur Leistungsmessung* orientieren sich an den Anforderungen für die Leistungsfeststellung am Gymnasium. Wie Sie wissen, legen aktuelle Lehrpläne ganz besonderen Wert auf Kompetenzorientierung und kommunikativen Anspruch. Darauf haben wir bei der Entwicklung dieses Hefts besonderen Wert gelegt, um Ihnen Aufgabenformate an die Hand zu geben, die auf dem neuesten Stand sind und sich daher optimal für die Erstellung von Klassenarbeiten eignen.

Aufbau

Kompetenzbereiche: Pro Unit werden Materialien für Klassenarbeiten zu *Listening*, *Reading*, *Writing*, *Mediation*, Grammatik und Wortschatz sowie *Speaking* angeboten. Entsprechend den unterschiedlichen Voraussetzungen einiger Bundesländer werden die Aufgaben zur *Grammatik* und zum *Wortschatz* getrennt angeboten. Diese Materialien können somit einfach nach Bedarf eingesetzt werden.
Die Aufgaben sind thematisch nach *Units* gegliedert, und folgen der Progression des Vokabulars im Schülerbuch. Das Symbol ▲ zeigt an, dass es sich bei der gekennzeichneten Aufgabe um eine vergleichsweise anspruchsvolle Aufgabe handelt.

Die beiliegende **CD-ROM** enthält alle Tests und Lösungen als PDF und in editierbarer Form. So können Aufgaben gezielt ausgewählt und die Klassenarbeit individuell zusammengestellt werden.
Auf der CD-ROM befinden sich zudem die Audiodateien und Filmsequenzen (jeweils mit Transkript) zu den Hörverstehen- bzw. Hör-/Sehverstehensaufgaben im Heft. Pro Unit bieten wir Ihnen auf der CD-ROM darüber hinaus einen Vordruck für eine Förderempfehlung an (s. u.).

Die sprachliche Fertigkeit **Speaking** kann anhand von drei Schritten getestet werden: *Warm-up* (kurzes L-S Gespräch), *monologue* und *dialogue*. Themenentsprechende *Monologue*- und *Dialogue-Speaking cards* sowie *Teacher's notes* finden Sie im Heft und auf der CD-ROM.

Materialien zur Förderempfehlung

Binnendifferenzierung und individuelle Förderung sind zentrale Bestandteile eines innovativen Fremdsprachenunterrichts, der die Bedürfnisse der einzelnen Schülerinnen und Schüler in den Mittelpunkt rückt und somit zu einem bestmöglichen individuellen Kompetenzaufbau beiträgt. Diese zentralen Bestandteile werden auch in den vorliegenden *Vorschläge zur Leistungsmessung* aufgegriffen. Auf der beiliegenden CD-ROM finden Sie pro Unit eine Förderempfehlung als PDF (für Unit 1 auf S. 3 auch in gedruckter Form) und auch als Word-Datei (editierbar), die es Ihnen ermöglicht, allen Schülerinnen und Schülern, die Förderbedarf im Bereich einzelner sprachlicher Fähigkeiten und Fertigkeiten aufweisen, eine gezielte Rückmeldung zu diesem Förderbedarf zu geben. Die Förderempfehlungen zeigen auf, was die Schülerinnen und Schüler in welchem Kompetenzbereich konkret aufarbeiten und wiederholen müssen, um ihren Förderbedarf auszugleichen. Darüber hinaus erfolgen ausgewählte Querverweise zu passenden Hilfestellungen (bspw. vertiefendes Übungsmaterial) in das Schülerbuch oder Workbook. Dieses Vorgehen ermöglicht nicht nur den Ausgleich des individuellen Förderbedarfs, sondern dient Ihren Schülerinnen und Schülern, deren Eltern und Ihnen auch als Grundlage der Dokumentation des Kompetenzaufbaus und der frühzeitigen Beseitigung von Lernhindernissen. Auf diese Weise erwerben Ihre Schülerinnen und Schüler auch methodische Kompetenzen, erlernen Techniken selbständigen und eigenverantwortlichen Lernens und nutzen die Förderempfehlungen als *advance organizers* zur Planung und Steuerung ihrer Lernprozesse.

Kommentar zur individuellen Förderung

Name:

Klasse:

Förderempfehlung:

	Diese Dinge haben nicht so gut geklappt:	Kompetenzbereich	Ausgewähltes Material zur Vertiefung und Wiederholung
☐	Ich muss noch üben, einem Text, den ich höre, Informationen zu entnehmen (Schwerpunkt: Ferienerlebnisse / Erlebnisbericht).	Hören	SB: S. 13/Text; S. 15/16; S. 16/18 WB: S. 3/3; S. 7/13
☐	Ich muss noch üben, einem Text, den ich lese, Informationen zu entnehmen (Schwerpunkt: Schulausflug; Erlebnisse englischer Schüler in Deutschland / Erlebnisbericht).	Lesen	SB: S. 10/1; S. 16/ 18; S. 19/2 WB: S. 9/17–18
☐	Ich muss mir noch einmal anschauen und trainieren, wie ich auf Grundlage von Bildern einen Bericht verfassen kann.	Schreiben	SB: S. 11/4; S. 17/22; S. 133/6; S. 135/13 WB: S. 8/16; S. 9/19
☐	Ich muss mir noch einmal anschauen und trainieren, wie ich einen Reisebericht schreiben kann.	Schreiben	SB: S. 12/7; S. 22–23/ Unit Task WB: S. 8/16
☐	Ich muss noch einmal wiederholen, wie ich über die Vor- und Nachteile von Ausflugszielen sprechen und in einer Diskussion eine Entscheidung für ein Ausflugsziel herbeiführen kann.	Sprechen	SB: S. 9/3; S. 16/18 WB: S. 10/23
☐	Ich muss noch einmal trainieren, wie ich den Inhalt einer deutschsprachigen Homepage über ein Ferienziel auf Englisch wiedergeben kann.	Mediation	SB: S. 12/8 WB: S. 7/12
☐	Ich muss die Vokabeln aus Unit 1 noch einmal wiederholen: ☐ Wortfeld Adjektive zur Personenbeschreibung ☐ Wortfeld *outdoor activities* ☐ weiteres Unit-Vokabular	Wortschatz	SB: S. 9/3; S. 16/18; S. 132/1; S. 134/7; S. 135/11, S. 202/Tabelle WB: S. 2/1–2; S. 9/18; S. 11/24–5
☐	Ich muss wiederholen, wie die einfache Vergangenheitsform (*simple past*) gebildet wird: ☐ regular verbs ☐ Verneinungen ☐ irregular verbs ☐ Kurzantworten ☐ Fragen	Grammatik	SB: S. 10/2; S. 11/3–5; S. 13/10; S. 14/11–14; S. 25/1–3; S. 132/3; S. 133/5; S. 134/7 WB: S. 3/4–5; S. 4/6; S. 5/8–9; S. 6/10–11
☐	Ich muss üben, wie ich Personen oder Dinge miteinander vergleichen kann: ☐ taller / the tallest ☐ taller / more exciting than ... ☐ more exciting / the most exciting ☐ (not) as tall / exciting as ...	Grammatik	SB: S. 16/19; S. 17/20–22; S. 25/4; S. 134/9; S. 135/10–12 WB: S. 8/14–15; S. 12/26

Weitere Anmerkungen:

Ich habe von der Klassenarbeit meines Sohnes/meiner Tochter und von der Förderempfehlung Kenntnis genommen.

_____
(Unterschrift einer/s Erziehungsberechtigten)

Green Line 2
Vorschläge zur Leistungsmessung
ISBN 978-3-12-834224-5

Inhalt des Hefts

Unit 1 My friends and I

LISTENING **1** **Listening: How were your holidays?**

Either:

a) *Listen to the dialogue and choose the best heading for this text:*

1. An exciting but dangerous holiday!
2. Home can be a dangerous place!
3. Gorge scrambling: A fun but dangerous sport!
4. A holiday at home!

Title: _____

b) *Listen. Are the statements true or false? Tick ✔ the correct answer.*

	true	false
1. Emily went to an outdoor centre with her family.	☐	☐
2. Emily enjoyed gorge scrambling.	☐	☐
3. They needed to climb a gorge before they could across the river.	☐	☐
4. A horse jumped into the river and the girl riding it fell into the water.	☐	☐
5. The day before the friends went home, they climbed a mountain.	☐	☐
6. The storm made climbing more dangerous for Emily.	☐	☐
7. Emily broke her foot on holiday.	☐	☐

▲ *Listen again and correct the wrong sentences.*

Or:

Listen and answer the questions in 1 to 5 words.

1. Where did Emily go in the holidays?_____

2. What activity did Emily do first? _____

3. How does she describe gorge scrambling? _____

4. What happened to a girl when her horse

   jumped into the river? _____

5. What happened when they climbed a mountain? _____

6. Why can't Emily walk now?_____

7. What place was the most dangerous for Emily?_____

Green Line 2
Vorschläge zur Leistungsmessung
ISBN 978-3-12-834224-5

2 Trouble on Red Nose Day

Either:

a) *Listen and put the correct pictures in the right order. Two pictures don't show what's in the story!*

b) *Answer the questions in 1 to 6 words.*

1. Why did the dog chase the boy? _____

2. Why did the boy give Samuel and Harry money? _____

_____

Or:

Listen. What do you find out about these people (or the dog)? Put the letters in the correct parts of the grid. More than one letter goes in every part. Sometimes one letter goes in more than one part.

Samuel and Harry:	The older boys:
The girl:	The dog:

a) chased the boy   b) one felt embarrassed   c) ran to the boy after he fell

d) collected money for charity   e) one ran away with the money   f) played saxophones

g) had a dog   h) were unfriendly   i) stayed till a boy said sorry and gave money

© Ernst Klett Verlag GmbH, Stuttgart 2015 | www.klett.de
Von dieser Druckvorlage ist die Vervielfältigung für den eigenen Unterrichtsgebrauch
gestattet. Die Kopiergebühren sind abgegolten. Alle Rechte vorbehalten.

Green Line 2
Vorschläge zur Leistungsmessung
ISBN 978-3-12-834224-5

READING **3** **Our school trip**

A Last July our class went to Germany. We were in the coach for a very long time, but we sang and played games and had a great time.

B When we got to Freiburg, we were all tired and a little nervous. Our host families[1] met us and took us home. Their houses were different from our houses in England – most were bigger. The food was a bit strange for us too!

C It was hot[2] while we were there – much hotter than in England – and so we often went to the outdoor swimming pool[3]. We also played lots of ball games and had picnics. It was great to be outside!

D On the first Saturday we went climbing in the mountains. That was exciting! When we went across what looked like a small river, five people fell in! Then we all jumped in and swam!

E The best thing was the football game on the last day. We played Germany against England. Guess who won? But they want to come and visit us and let us try again!

F We were all sad when we said goodbye to our new German friends. We had a great time in Germany. Many things were different there. Their swimming pools were more fun and the weather was better, but we were all happy to be home and eat our good English food!

1 **host family** Gastfamilie | 2 **hot** heiß | 3 **outdoor swimming pool** Freibad

Either:

a) *Read the text and choose a heading for each part. There is one extra heading.*

1. Not everything was better _____

2. Long but not boring _____

3. The worst time of all _____

4. A trip to England _____

5. Adventure in the mountains _____

6. A home away from home _____

7. Fun and great weather _____

▲ **b)** *Draw a grid to show the six parts of the text and the main ideas in each part.*

Or:

Read the text and answer the questions in 1 to 6 words.

1. How did the class get to Germany? _____

2. How did the kids feel when they got to Freiburg? _____

3. What did they do when it was hot? _____

4. They swam in a pool and also in … _____

5. Who won the football match? _____

6. What four things were different in Germany? _____

7. What did they think about the German food? _____

Green Line 2
Vorschläge zur Leistungsmessung
ISBN 978-3-12-834224-5

READING **4** **We were all winners**

Dear Jenny,

I can't believe it. They won! I don't know what happened. Our idea was much better than their idea. We made cakes and sold them at school. The kids bought all of them! We made £54, but Kate's group made more money. I don't like Kate. She always wins. I'm a better singer than she is, but she always wins the talent contest. Why?

They sold hot[1] drinks at the market. OK, it was a good idea. It's cold now, and lots of people wanted a hot drink. I bought a drink too, and they were good, but they weren't anything special. They just made some hot fruit drinks and some teas and sold them. Of course, they were more expensive than our cakes. And lots of people just gave them some money.

We did our best. We wore red noses and we tried to do funny things – they didn't – and people laughed. Jack said I was the silliest person at school! I'm not sure if that was nice or not. I know the money goes to charity and so we were all winners in the end, but I really wanted to make more money than she did. I wanted to win just once!

Love, Emily

1 **hot** heiß

Either:

a) *Read the statements. True or false? Tick ✔ the correct answer.*

	true	false
1. Kate and Jenny raised money for charity together.	☐	☐
2. Emily made cakes and sold them all.	☐	☐
3. Kate and Emily are good friends.	☐	☐
4. The hot drinks Kate's group sold were very special.	☐	☐
5. Emily bought something from Kate.	☐	☐
6. Emily's group tried to be funny so people laughed.	☐	☐
7. Kate's group made more money than Emily's group.	☐	☐

▲ **b)** *Listen again and correct the wrong sentences.*

Or:

Read the text and make notes about Kate and Emily in the boxes.

	Kate	Emily
1. How did they make money?		
2. Where did they make money?		
3. What did they do extra to win?		
4. How much money did they raise?		
5. Who never wins, and why isn't it fair?		

Green Line 2
Vorschläge zur Leistungsmessung
ISBN 978-3-12-834224-5

WRITING **5** **Red Nose Day**

How was Red Nose Day for Jay, Luke, Holly and Olivia? Look at the pictures and write about their day (6 to 8 sentences). You can start like this:

After the four friends made lots of money for Comic Relief ...

_____

_____

_____

_____

_____

WRITING **6** **A travel report**

Write about your last school trip (6 to 8 sentences).

Write about:
- where you went.
- when you went there.
- what you did there.
- how it was. (What happened? Did you enjoy it? Why/why not?)

Or use the notes and write about Sophie's school trip last year (6 to 8 sentences).

- Where: the Black Mountains in Wales
- When: May
- What: went mountain climbing; went canoeing *(Kanufahren)*; walked in the forest; saw animals
- Weather: nice below, colder high up *(hoch oben)*
- What happened? Did you enjoy it? Why/why not?

_____

_____

_____

_____

_____

Green Line 2
Vorschläge zur Leistungsmessung
ISBN 978-3-12-834224-5

7 More than a holiday!

You want to go on holiday with your English friends. You find this information on the internet, but they need your help to understand it. Answer their questions. Be careful! One of the answers isn't in the text!

Egal, ob du schon wie ein Jockey reitest oder noch Anfänger bist, wir haben den richtigen Reitkurs für dich! Bist du 13 oder älter?
Teenager können ohne ihre Eltern kommen. Unsere Betreuer sind nicht nur gut ausgebildet, sie bieten dir auch spannende Erlebnisse an einem der schönsten Orte Deutschlands. Bei uns gibt es tolle Ferienangebote, da wird es garantiert nicht langweilig! Erkunde die Gegend bei geführten Ausritten durch unsere faszinierende Bergwelt.

Noch nicht genug Action? Keine Sorge – bei uns gibt es jede Menge!
Du kannst z.B. auch Kajak fahren oder bergsteigen! Abends hast du die Wahl, ob du dich in unserem Partyraum auf der Tanzfläche vergnügst oder den Tag gemütlich bei einem Film ausklingen lässt!

Chris: I like to ride horses but I'm not very good at it. Is that a problem?

You: _____

Tina: What's that about teenagers and 13? We're 13 years old!

You: _____

Chris: Where can you ride the horses?

You: _____

Chris: You can ride alone in the mountains? That's dangerous!

You: _____

Chris: I see that you can also go kayaking. What else can you do there?

You: _____

Tina: And what can you do in the evening?

You: _____

Tina: What else is nice about the place?

You: _____

Chris: OK, it sounds good, but how do we get there?

You: _____

Green Line 2
Vorschläge zur Leistungsmessung
ISBN 978-3-12-834224-5

8 A report about Red Nose Day → (after Station 1)

Write the correct words in the gaps in this e-mail. There are two extra words.

> best | caught | pyjamas | raised | report | sale | yearbook | embarrassing | proud of | shy

Hi Alice,

Can you write a _____ about Red Nose Day for our _____? I've got some

good photos, but we need a short text to go with them. We _____ £2,500 this

year, which was better than last year. Many classes had some great ideas, but 6a's idea was

the _____,

I think. Their _____ of old computer games and phones raised lots of money.

I got some good photos of teachers in costume, and I _____ Mr Hansen on camera. I'm

very _____ that picture! Can you believe he wore his _____?

See you tomorrow! Jake

9 Look what happened! → (after Station 2)

A lot went wrong on this class trip! Who are these people, or what are these things or parts of the body?
Put the correct words next to the numbers. You see the first letter of each word.

1. f _____
2. c _____
3. d _____
4. p _____
5. t _____
6. e _____
7. n _____
8. m _____
9. p _____

© Ernst Klett Verlag GmbH, Stuttgart 2015 | www.klett.de
Von dieser Druckvorlage ist die Vervielfältigung für den eigenen Unterrichtsgebrauch
gestattet. Die Kopiergebühren sind abgegolten. Alle Rechte vorbehalten.

Green Line 2
Vorschläge zur Leistungsmessung
ISBN 978-3-12-834224-5

11

VOCABULARY **10** A puzzle → (after Station 3)

Across

4. I'm … about the test tomorrow.
6. He's very … – he can talk to anybody.
7. It isn't easy – it's …
8. I don't like it when there are lots of people I don't know. I'm …
9. Watch your head. The door is …
10. I was very … when I walked into the wrong class.

Down

1. That wasn't a dream, it was …
2. I'm sure I can do it. Yes, I'm …
3. She's very … Maybe 1 metre 80?
5. Who sent the letter? – I don't know. It's …
7. That mountain is … – it must be 2,000 metres.

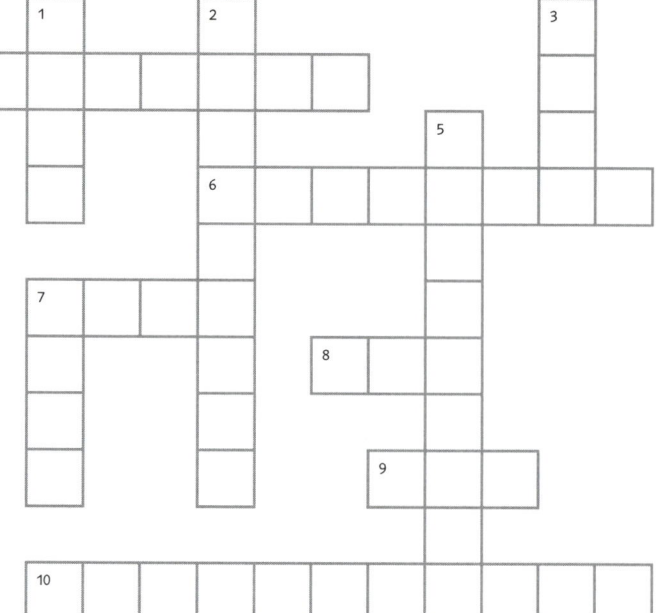

LANGUAGE **11** Red Nose Day – A great idea! → (after Station 1)

What did Olivia's class do on Red Nose Day? Complete the sentences with verbs in the simple past.

I love Red Nose Day and I love to raise money for charity – it's always great fun. Last year

I _____ (make) and _____ (sell) cakes, and I _____ (sing) in a

comedy show with some friends in the streets. We _____ (wear) red noses. This year

I _____ (want) to do something different, but what? I _____ (think), but

no good ideas _____ (come) to me. Then one day I _____ (see) an older

neighbour. She _____ (be) in the garden and I _____ (chat) to her for some

time. She _____ (have) lots of work to do and she _____ (need) some help,

so I _____ (help) her, of course. When I _____ (finish), she wanted to give me

some money, and that was when I had my idea. So this year all my class _____ (start) a

club called: "Garden work for charity". We _____ (do) lots of work and

_____ (raise) lots of money and in the end we _____ (be) all happy.

Green Line 2
Vorschläge zur Leistungsmessung
ISBN 978-3-12-834224-5

LANGUAGE **12** **Adventure holiday** → (after Station 2)

Molly and Chris' last school trip was an adventure holiday. Use the tips and give short answers for the questions. (✔) = yes and (✗) = no

1. Was Molly excited about the holiday? (✔) _____.

2. Did Chris climb a mountain too? (✗) _____

3. But Chris swam across the river, right? (✗) _____

4. Were Molly and Chris in the same group? (✔) _____

5. Was the weather good during their holiday? (✔) _____

6. Did Chris help Molly when they were gorge scrambling? (✗)_____

7. Was the teacher happy about this? (✗) _____

LANGUAGE **13** **What a joke!** → (after Station 2)

Olivia did an interview with Terry, who went to her school a few years ago. To raise money for Red Nose Day, Terry told jokes to people in the street. Complete Olivia's questions. Remember to use question words.

Olivia: You raised a lot of money! _____ you successful[1], do you think?

Terry: I was successful because my jokes were funny for everyone!

Olivia: _____ get the idea to do this?

Terry: I got the idea after I a lot of friends told me that I can tell great jokes.

Olivia: _____ do your comedy show?

Terry: I did it in front of the main train station, where there are lots of people!

Olivia: _____ you there?

Terry: I was there the whole day! I was really tired at the end, but I had a great time!

Olivia: And _____ raise with your jokes?

Terry: I raised £300.

Olivia: That's great! _____ do so that people gave you so much?

Terry: First I asked them what kind of jokes *they* like to hear. Then I found the right joke for them!

[1] **successful** erfolgreich

Green Line 2
Vorschläge zur Leistungsmessung
ISBN 978-3-12-834224-5

LANGUAGE **14** **Horses at the adventure centre** → (after Station 3)

a) *Complete the gaps in the text and compare Megan with Paddy and Silver.*

Possible words for comparing	Megan	Paddy	Silver
tall/big/small (size)	15.2 hands	17.1 hands	16 hands
expensive/cheap	£5,000	£3,500	£2,000
old/young	5 years	14 years	6 months

Megan cost £5,000, so she's _____! If you compare her price to the others, she's the

_____ horse here. She's good with children, and at 15.2 hands she's the

_____ of the three horses. Megan is still a _____ horse

at five years old, so she's _____ than Paddy, but not as _____ as Silver.

▲ **b)** *Now write six sentences about the other two horses.*

LANGUAGE **15** **Who was the bravest?** → (after Station 3)

Complete the sentences with the adjective in the correct form.

Our class went to an outdoor centre in Wales in October. The weather there is often

_____ (bad) than in any other part of the UK, but when we were there it was

_____ (nice) than it usually is. I love outdoor activities so I had a great time, but some people

didn't enjoy it as much. Lisa was the _____ (nervous) person in the whole group. She was

scared of lots of activities, but she thought mountain climbing was the _____ (awful). I was

the _____ (good) at climbing in the group, and I liked gorge scrambling too, but I don't

think it's as fun as climbing. Lisa had real problems with the gorge. We decided to walk over a tree to

get across a river. It wasn't _____ (high) than two metres over the water, but Lisa was so

scared that she wanted to go back. We told Lisa it wasn't as _____ (scary) as it looked and

she got _____ (confident). We talked to her, and I walked back to her and helped her for the

last two or three metres. She did it and she was _____ (happy) than the rest of us.

Later I asked the teacher who the _____ (brave) person was on this holiday.

"Lisa was _____ (brave) than any of you," he said.

Green Line 2
Vorschläge zur Leistungsmessung
ISBN 978-3-12-834224-5

Unit 2 Let's discover TTS!

1 The Sign Language Club

Either:

a) *Listen. Which signs can you learn in the Sign Language Club in the first year? Tick* ✔ *four boxes.*

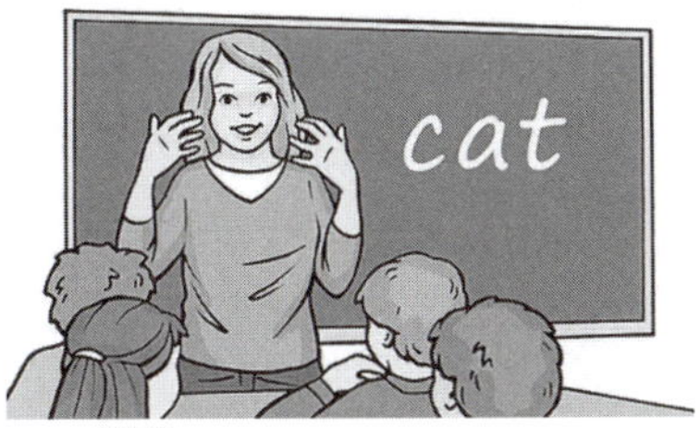

cat 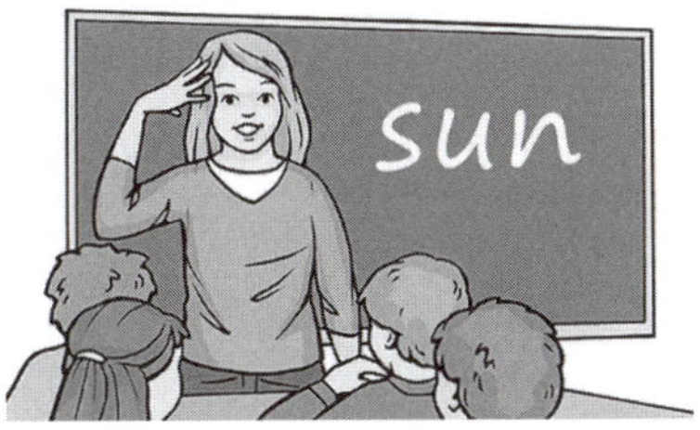 ☐   sun 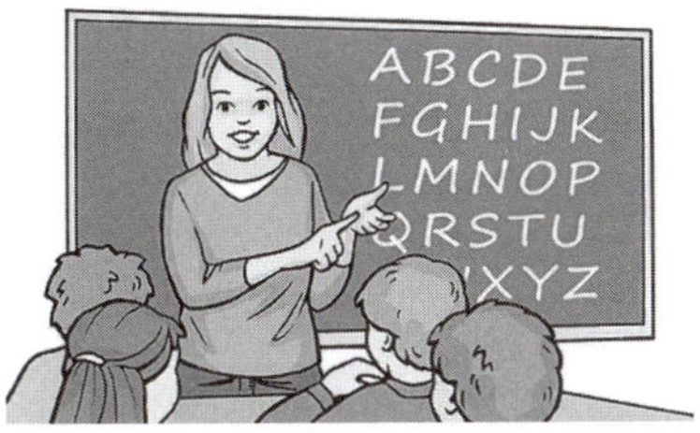 ☐   the alphabet ☐

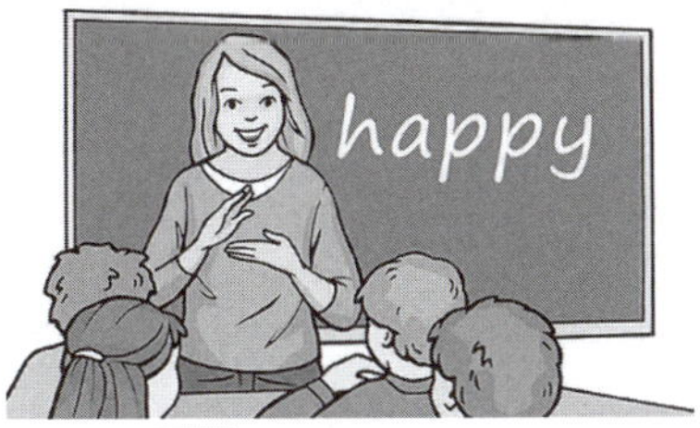

happy 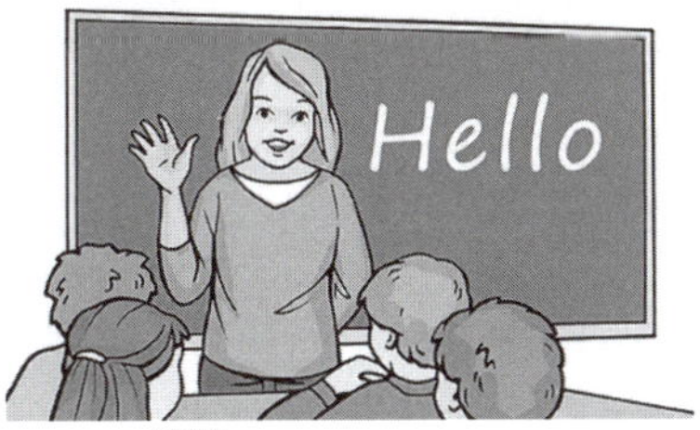 ☐   Hello! 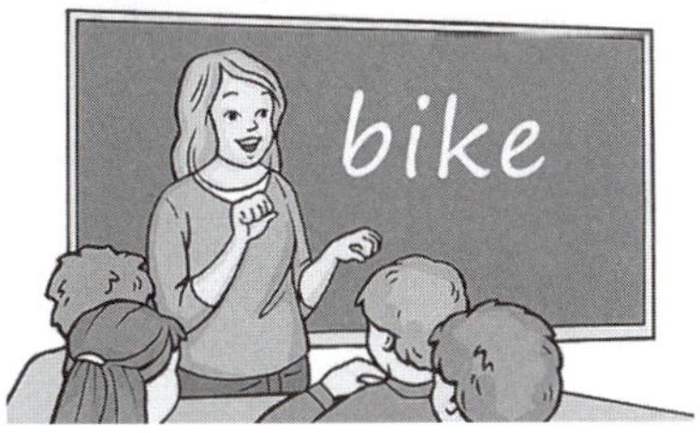 ☐   bike ☐

b) *Listen again. Are the statements true or false? Tick* ✔ *the correct answer.*	true	false
1. Ben is presenting the Sign Language Club, which is three years old.	☐	☐
2. An older student shows the club members how to use sign language.	☐	☐
3. Julie uses sign language with her brother.	☐	☐
4. The students usually make the signs right the first time they try them.	☐	☐
5. The club meets on Wednesdays in the lunch break.	☐	☐

Or:

Listen and answer the questions in 2 to 7 words.

1. When did the Sign Language Club start? _____

2. What is the most useful thing you can learn? _____

3. Which of these things **doesn't** Julie say that you learn the signs for in the first year?

    the days   the months   the colours   the weather _____

4. Why did Julie learn sign language? _____

5. Why do they laugh a lot? _____

6. When is the club? _____

Green Line 2
Vorschläge zur Leistungsmessung
ISBN 978-3-12-834224-5

2 Using a timetable

Either:

Listen. Complete the new timetable with the correct information.

Monday	Subject	Room	Why?
8:50	Technology	1.	2.
9:50	3.	T17	
10:50	**Break**		
11:10	4.	G40	5.
12:10	6.	B12	7.
13:10	**Lunch**		
14:00	Dance	Studio B	8.

Or:

Listen and choose the correct answer(s).There can be more than one answer.

1. The information is for …

   a) ☐ today.

   b) ☐ every Monday.

   c) ☐ next Monday.

2. Last week the students…

   a) ☐ made films and watched them.

   b) ☐ made films. They want to watch them this week.

   c) ☐ made films. They can watch them next week.

3. The second technology lesson is at …

   a) ☐ 9:15.

   b) ☐ 9:50.

   c) ☐ 9:30.

4. The Maths class is moving to …

   a) ☐ G40.

   b) ☐ G14.

   c) ☐ D40.

5. The Drama class is moving because …

   a) ☐ they need more tables.

   b) ☐ they need computers.

   c) ☐ they are making costumes.

6. Studio A …

   a) ☐ has a broken window.

   b) ☐ is where Dance is next Monday.

   c) ☐ is where Dance usually takes place.

© Ernst Klett Verlag GmbH, Stuttgart 2015 | www.klett.de
Von dieser Druckvorlage ist die Vervielfältigung für den eigenen Unterrichtsgebrauch
gestattet. Die Kopiergebühren sind abgegolten. Alle Rechte vorbehalten.

Green Line 2
Vorschläge zur Leistungsmessung
ISBN 978-3-12-834224-5

READING **3** **A History project**

Holly, Luke and Dave were having lunch in a museum café and talking about their school projects.

"Which historical person did you choose for your project, Luke?" asked Holly.

"Thomas Tallis," answered Luke. "I thought it was a great idea but I think I need to choose another person. I can't find enough information. He's very famous for his church music, but I can't really tell you much more. There are no paintings of him – nothing!"

"I think I was lucky then," said Dave. "I chose Sir Francis Drake and there is *a lot* of information about him. He was one of the most famous men in England when Elizabeth I was Queen and he was the first English man to sail[1] around the world. He brought back lots of things like new foods and jewellery. When his ship came back to Greenwich, the Queen made him a knight[2]."

Sir Francis Drake

"Very interesting, but I think *I* chose the best person!" said Holly. "I chose Samuel Pepys. He only lived in Greenwich for a year or so, but he wrote a very famous diary[3], which is full of information about London life in the 1600s. Pepys wrote about his friends and neighbours *and* about important historical events like the Great Fire[4] in 1666. London was very different after the fire ...".

"Enough!" said Luke. "Now who can *I* find out about?"

1 **sail** segeln | 2 **knight** Ritter | 3 **diary** Tagebuch | 4 **fire** Feuer

Either:

Read the text and say which person each sentence is about: Thomas Tallis, Sir Francis Drake or Samuel Pepys.

1. He lived in Greenwich for a year. _____

2. The Queen made him a knight in Greenwich. _____

3. He's famous for his church music. _____

4. He wrote about people and events in London. _____

5. There aren't any paintings of him. _____

6. He was the first English man to sail around the world. _____

Or:

Read the text and answer the questions in 2 to 8 words.

1. What is Luke's problem with the project? _____

2. What kind of music did Thomas Tallis write? _____

3. What did Sir Francis Drake do as the first English man? _____

4. What did Francis Drake bring back with him? _____

5. Who and what did Samuel Pepys write about (three things)? _____

Green Line 2
Vorschläge zur Leistungsmessung
ISBN 978-3-12-834224-5

4 Which club?

A Photo Club

Each week, we look at famous photos and discuss why they are good. Then we go outside and take photos – the wildlife garden is a great place for ideas! We also learn to take photos that are hard to do, like inside a very old, dark building. These photos are sometimes the best! In June and December there's a club display of all your photos so your friends can vote for their favourite - of course, there's a prize for the most popular picture!

B Dance Club

Learn a new dance each week! Then invite your friends and family to the end of year dance show and see how impressed they are! We also need people to help with costumes. Of course, we love to go to dance events in London, but these are expensive, so we only go once a year.

C Cooking Club

This year, we are learning how to make food from different parts of the world. We're starting with Italy – we hope you love pizza and pasta – and then we explore food from France and other countries. Each week, we give you a list of what you need to bring the next Monday. Please remember to bring a bag or box to take extra food home in. We always make more than we eat!

Either:

Read the text and tick ✔ *the club each sentence is about.*

	A	B	C
1. We go to London one time a year.	☐	☐	☐
2. This is a good club for you if you're hungry!	☐	☐	☐
3. You can get ideas from nature.	☐	☐	☐
4. You learn something about other countries.	☐	☐	☐
5. There's a competition two times a year.	☐	☐	☐
6. Please help us with our event!	☐	☐	☐

Or:

a) *Read the text. Are the statements true or false? Tick* ✔ *the correct answer.*

	true	false
1. At the Photo Club, your friends can help you win something.	☐	☐
2. It's easy to take good photos where it's dark.	☐	☐
3. At the Dance Club you learn different dances every month.	☐	☐
4. Trips to dance shows in London cost a lot of money.	☐	☐
5. You don't need to bring anything to the Cooking Club.	☐	☐
6. In this club you learn to make food from one country.	☐	☐

▲ **b)** *Correct the wrong sentences.*

Green Line 2
Vorschläge zur Leistungsmessung
ISBN 978-3-12-834224-5

5 Partner school

Your school is trying to find an English partner school for an exchange programme (Austauschprogramm). Your aunt in England tells you that the school in her town is looking for a German partner school. Write an e-mail to this school and try to make them interested in your school. Write six sentences and think about the following things:

- what subjects there are and which ones you think are best (give reasons)
- some of the clubs they can join and what people do there
- some of the sports people can play

Dear Mrs Brown,

My aunt told me that you are looking for a German partner school for your

exchange programme. This is why I'm writing to you to tell you about our school.

6 School trips and stories

a) *Imagine that you are a student in Holly and Dave's class. There can be only one class trip this year and all of you have to vote tomorrow! Look at the suggestions below. Write an e-mail to Holly or Dave and tell him/her which trip you like best and why. Write six sentences.*

▲ **b)** *Write a story with the title "A crazy school day".*

Green Line 2
Vorschläge zur Leistungsmessung
ISBN 978-3-12-834224-5

7 School clubs

Your class and a class in England are exchanging information about the clubs at your schools. Use the information below from your school's website and write an e-mail to them in English where you describe the clubs in your own words.

In unserer Schule gibt es fünfzehn AGs. Einige finden sogar in der Mittagspause statt. In der Buch-AG (mittwochs um 12 Uhr) schlägt jede Woche jemand ein neues Buch vor und alle lesen es bis zum nächsten Mal. Dann diskutieren alle über das Buch und sagen, was sie davon halten. Die beliebteste AG ist der Schülerzeitschrifts-AG (donnerstags um 13 Uhr). Zuerst entscheiden sich die Mitglieder, welche Artikel und Fotos sie verwenden wollen. Dann führen sie Interviews, schreiben Artikel, machen lustige Fotos ... Alle lesen unsere Zeitschrift sehr gern!

Hi students in 6B! You've got some great clubs at your school! We do too! ...

_____

_____

_____

_____

_____

8 A school trip!

Holly wrote to Pia about her class trip to the art museum. Pia wants to tell her cousin (whose English isn't good) about it in her e-mail, but Pia doesn't know every word in English. Help Pia write this part of the e-mail in German. If you don't know a word, try to guess what it is. Is it like a German word? Can you use the context (the words around it) to guess the meaning?

Some of my classmates weren't interested because they didn't understand what they were looking at (it was modern art). But I thought that some of the pictures were cool and I liked the colours and designs. I was concentrating on one picture when suddenly Jay ran into me (he didn't notice me because he was talking to Luke) and pushed me, and I stepped over the line in front of the picture! Then an alarm rang! The museum guard who was watching the people in the gallery ran to me and our teacher did too! They were very upset. But Jay and I explained that we weren't trying to make trouble and we said that we were very sorry! They told us to be more careful.

Hollys Besuch im Kunstmuseum mit ihrer Klasse war sehr aufregend! ...

_____

_____

_____

Green Line 2
Vorschläge zur Leistungsmessung
ISBN 978-3-12-834224-5

9 **What we do in lessons** → (after Station 1)

Find the correct ending for each sentence and write the number in the box.

1. We can choose basketball or volleyball
2. We sometimes have to learn a poem
3. We do really fun things on computers
4. We do experiments
5. We show the pictures that we paint
6. We learn about life in the past
7. We learn about numbers

a) ☐ in Technology lessons.
b) ☐ in Science lessons.
c) ☐ in History lessons.
d) ☐ in Maths lessons.
f) ☐ in English lessons.
g) ☐ in PE lessons.
h) ☐ in Art lessons.

10 **Club flyers** → (after Station 2)

Look at these parts of club flyers. Which of the words below belong in which flyer?
There are two extra words.

wildlife | interested | offer | Birdwatching | paintings | Architect |
welcome | dancers | Eco | Fashion | started | forward | steal

1. Do you like to _____ the show? Then join the Drama Club!

2. Are you _____ in birds? Our _____ Club is on Friday at

   lunchtime.

3. Can you write interesting articles? Then _____ to the Magazine Club!

4. Come and take a look at the Art Club _____ in the Art room.

5. Do you love to talk about buildings? Then come to the _____ Club!

6. Do you look _____ to the end of year shows? Come to Singing Club and you

   can be part of the fun!

7. We need people to join our Dance Club *now*! Calling all _____! Let's get

   _____!

8. Do you love to work outside with _____? The _____

   Club needs you!

Green Line 2
Vorschläge zur Leistungsmessung
ISBN 978-3-12-834224-5

LANGUAGE **11** **The Science Museum** → (after Station 1)

*Read the text and write **who/that**, **which/that** or **whose** in the gaps.*

Last week we went on a great visit to the new Science Museum _____ opened last year.

It was different from other museums – you could do experiments and take photos! The teacher

_____ came with us put us into teams and we all had to find different things. My team had

to find things _____ help us move through the world. The team _____

my friend was in found lots of good things for nature. The third team's job was to find things

_____ people used or still use to communicate (*kommunizieren*) with each other.

Our team was really fast – we had one girl _____ father works at the museum, so she

knows where everything is! We took photos and next day in class we talked about them. The team

_____ photos were the best won a prize – and that was our team!

LANGUAGE **12** **We won!** → (after Station 1)

*Luke is writing an e-mail to a friend about a school football game. Join the sentences with **who/that**, **which/that**, or **whose**.*

1. The other players were from West London. We were playing against them.

   _____

2. The other team had a captain. His name was Will.

   _____

3. They wore football shoes. They were red and white.

   _____

4. The football shoes were yellow and blue. Our team wore them.

   _____

5. The students were from our school. Their cheering (*Jubel*) helped us play better!

   _____

6. We have a great captain. He always knows what to do.

   _____

Green Line 2
Vorschläge zur Leistungsmessung
ISBN 978-3-12-834224-5

LANGUAGE **13** **The show** → (after Station 1)

Olivia is talking about a show she and her friends were in for Red Nose Day.

a) *Write **who/that** or **which/that** in the gaps.*

1. We sang three songs _____ we learned this year.

2. There were other students _____ danced while we were singing.

3. They wore costumes _____ were purple and green.

4. I played a saxophone part _____ I wrote for the show.

5. A teacher _____ plays the guitar *(Gitarre)* helped us too.

6. The people _____ came to watch didn't want to go home!

b) *In two of the sentences, you don't need to use **who** or **which**. Which ones?*

LANGUAGE **14** **What were they doing?** → (after Station 2)

Holly, Olivia, Luke, Dave, Jay and Gwen were in the school playground at the end of break time. Write sentences about what was happening then.

1. Luke _____.

2. Olivia _____.

3. Jay _____.

4. Dave _____.

5. Gwen _____.

6. A bird _____ a nest.

7. The sun _____.

© Ernst Klett Verlag GmbH, Stuttgart 2015 | www.klett.de
Von dieser Druckvorlage ist die Vervielfältigung für den eigenen Unterrichtsgebrauch
gestattet. Die Kopiergebühren sind abgegolten. Alle Rechte vorbehalten.

Green Line 2
Vorschläge zur Leistungsmessung
ISBN 978-3-12-834224-5

LANGUAGE **15** **A Technology lesson** → (after Station 2)

Dave and the others talk about the Technology lesson. Use the correct form of the past progressive.

Dave: That was a fun lesson. But why were you late, Luke?

Luke: I _____ (walk) to school when I remembered that my homework was

on the kitchen table, So I hurried back home. I was lucky – when I got to school, Mr Walker

_____ (show) Jay a website, so he didn't see me walk in late!

Holly: Which website _____ (he/show) you, Jay?

Jay: It was about bottle design. Our task was to design a bottle for apple juice. When Luke came,

we _____ (ask) Mr Walker some questions, so he didn't notice him.

We _____ (design) our bottle when the lesson ended (*vorbei war*).

We _____ (not work) very fast because there was so much to

think about!

Dave: Like is it nice to look at? Is it strong? What about recycling?

Olivia: And what _____ (you/do) when the lesson ended, Luke?

Dave: He _____ (not do) anything!

Luke: That's not true! I _____ (think) about the design too!

LANGUAGE **16** **Scary ghosts!** → (after Station 2)

▲ *Holly and Olivia went to the cinema last Saturday. Holly is telling another friend about it. Put the verbs in the simple past or past progressive form.*

We went to see "Ghost in the House" last Saturday. I _____ (not want) to go because,

as you know, I'm scared of ghosts! But everyone at school _____ (talk) about it

while they were at lunch last Friday, and then Olivia wanted to go. Her Mum took us by car, and while

we _____ (go), sometimes Olivia _____ (make) silly ghost noises

to scare me. I _____ (not be) scared at the beginning. I _____

(laugh) for the first five minutes while Olivia _____ (talk) like the actor! I

_____ (watch) the film when scary music started to play, and then I was scared! And

when we first _____ (see) the ghost, we _____ (jump) out of our

chairs! I couldn't watch after that!

Klett © Ernst Klett Verlag GmbH, Stuttgart 2015 | www.klett.de
Von dieser Druckvorlage ist die Vervielfältigung für den eigenen Unterrichtsgebrauch
gestattet. Die Kopiergebühren sind abgegolten. Alle Rechte vorbehalten.

Green Line 2
Vorschläge zur Leistungsmessung
ISBN 978-3-12-834224-5

Unit 3 London is amazing!

LISTENING **1** **Holiday plans**

Either:

Luke is excited about the holidays but Dave isn't. Listen to their conversation and complete the sentences in 1 to 7 words.

1. Dave isn't excited about his aunt and uncle's visit because

   _____

   _____

   _____

2. They want to see all the _____ like Buckingham Palace again.

3. Luke's plans for the holidays are to _____ and to go to the

   London Comic Con.

4. One thing you can do at the London Comic Con is _____

5. The tickets that Luke wants to buy cost _____

6. At the end Dave thinks the holidays are going to be OK because he _____

   _____ with Luke.

Or:

a) *Luke is excited but Dave isn't! Listen to their conversation.*
   True or false? Tick ✔ the correct answer.

	true	false
1. Dave is going to stay with his aunt and uncle during the holidays.	☐	☐
2. Dave's aunt and uncle don't want to see Buckingham Palace again.	☐	☐
3. Luke plans to see a football game.	☐	☐
4. Dave wants to see a football game too.	☐	☐
5. Dave wants to find out more about the London Comic Con.	☐	☐
6. At the London Comic Con you can even see famous people.	☐	☐
7. Dave knew from the beginning that his holidays weren't going to be boring.	☐	☐

 b) *Listen again and correct the wrong sentences.*

Green Line 2
Vorschläge zur Leistungsmessung
ISBN 978-3-12-834224-5

2   A tour of London

Either:

Listen and choose the correct answer(s). More than one answer can be correct.

1. Buckingham Palace has _____ rooms.

    a) ☐ 577

    b) ☐ 757

    c) ☐ 775

2. You can visit parts of the palace in …

    a) ☐ August

    b) ☐ September

    c) ☐ November

3. This bus tour ends at …

    a) ☐ the Science Museum.

    b) ☐ Buckingham Palace.

    c) ☐ Westminster Cathedral.

4. How old is Hyde Park?

    a) ☐ almost 500 years old

    b) ☐ almost 900 years old

    c) ☐ 1,500 years old

5. What is true about Hyde Park?

    a) ☐ It's one of London's smallest parks.

    b) ☐ You can go swimming there.

    c) ☐ Its lake is only for swimming.

6. You can listen to concerts here.

    a) ☐ Hyde Park

    b) ☐ Buckingham Palace

    c) ☐ Royal Albert Hall

Or:

a) *Listen. Where does the bus stop on this tour? Put numbers beside the places to show the order of the tour bus stops. Be careful! Two stops aren't on this tour!*

Westminster Cathedral _____   Buckingham Palace _____

Victoria and Albert Museum _____   St James's Palace _____

Royal Albert Hall _____   Hyde Park _____   Science Museum _____

b) *Answer these questions in 1 to 5 words.*

1. How many rooms does Buckingham Palace have? _____

2. What else does Buckingham Palace have? _____

3. How much does it cost to visit Buckingham Palace? _____

4. How old is Hyde Park? _____

5. What is Hyde Park famous for? _____

6. In which year did the Royal Albert Hall open? _____

Green Line 2
Vorschläge zur Leistungsmessung
ISBN 978-3-12-834224-5

READING

3 A trip to Hampton Court Palace[1]

"Look at this website! It says there are ghosts at Hampton Court," Holly said to Olivia. Olivia thought this was interesting, so she asked her dad, Desmond, to take them there. Olivia's dad was happy to take the whole family because he loved to visit historical places. He took Holly too, because she was also interested in ghosts.

When they got to the palace, they found Catherine Howard's old rooms. She was King Henry the Eighth's fifth wife, and there was a famous ghost story about her.

"Why did the king's men cut her head off[2]?" asked Olivia as she looked at a picture of her.

"He probably just wanted a new wife," answered Desmond.

"It was awful! That's why some say she comes back as a ghost. They call her the *Screaming Lady*," Holly whispered quietly to Olivia. But Lucy heard her too, and she was scared. At that moment, they heard a horrible[3] scream. "Did you hear that? That's Catherine Howard!" Holly said excitedly. Lucy screamed and ran away. Then Holly saw a strange white woman and screamed too!

"Holly, I'm sure it's just an actor," said Desmond, "Don't worry!" He went to get Lucy.

Holly saw an actor in costume a minute later and asked, "Ah, excuse me … Did you just scream?"

"No, of course not! I didn't hear anything like that!" she said. "Who screamed?"

1 **palace** Palast | 2 **to cut off** *hier:* jmdn. köpfen | 3 **horrible** schrecklich, furchtbar

Either:

Read the text. Match the sentence parts. Put the correct letters next to the numbers below.

1. Desmond wants to go to the palace because
2. Holly wants to visit the palace because
3. Desmond says the King didn't want Catherine Howard to be his wife any more because
4. Catherine Howard became a ghost because
5. Lucy screams and runs away because
6. Holly screams because
7. Desmond isn't worried by the scream because
8. The actor is surprised because

a) she saw what looked like a woman's ghost.
b) she didn't hear anyone scream.
c) he thinks it was an actor.

d) she's interested in ghosts.
e) he's interested in history.
f) she hears someone screaming.
g) the king's men cut her head off.
h) he probably wanted a new wife.

1. _____   2. _____   3. _____   4. _____   5. _____   6. _____   7. _____   8. _____

Or:

a) *Read the text. Who is it? Write down the name. Sometimes more than one answer is possible.*

1. interested in ghosts _____
2. interested in history _____

3. comes back as a ghost _____
4. wanted another wife _____

5. scared by *(von)* a noise _____
6. sees something scary _____

7. didn't hear the scream _____

 b) *Why is the ending surprising? Explain in your own words.*

Green Line 2
Vorschläge zur Leistungsmessung
ISBN 978-3-12-834224-5

4 Lots of fun in London with just a little money

Sightseeing in London can be expensive but it doesn't have to be. Sights like castles and wax museums aren't cheap, but does that mean that you have to stay home and be bored?

No! If you haven't got much money, why not visit a museum! They aren't just for school trips, and many of them are free! Here's an example: Go to South Kensington and you can find three fantastic museums all near each other. They're all free, so you can visit each one.

The Natural History Museum is for anybody who is interested in animals and plants[1]. Most people's favourites are, of course, the dinosaurs.

The Victoria and Albert Museum is an art gallery, but is not only for those interested in art. There is also a great display on fashion and design through history.

The Science Museum is for everybody! It is one of the most popular science museums in Europe and can show you (nearly) everything you want to know about science and technology: past, present and future[2]. The displays are not just to look at; you can try lots of things yourself. And you can bring a sandwich and have a picnic!

Maybe you do only have a little money, but that doesn't mean you need to be bored in London!

1 **plant** Pflanze | 2 **future** Zukunft

Either:

a) *Read the text and tick* ✔ *the correct answer.*

	true	false
1. You can't go sightseeing in London if you don't have a lot of money.	☐	☐
2. You needn't pay to go in lots of museums.	☐	☐
3. South Kensington is an excellent museum.	☐	☐
4. The Natural History Museum has only got things which lived long ago.	☐	☐
5. The Victoria and Albert Museum isn't for people who are interested in art.	☐	☐
6. Most people like the Science Museum.	☐	☐

▲ **b)** *Read the text again and correct the wrong sentences.*

Or:

Read the text and answer the questions in 1 to 6 words. One answer isn't in the text. Put – here.

1. Which things cost a lot to visit in London? _____

2. When do teenagers usually visit museums? _____

3. What can you say about the three museums in South Kensington? _____

4. Which museum in London is only about modern things? _____

5. Where can you find out about clothes? _____

6. Where can you learn about the cars of yesterday, today and tomorrow? _____

Green Line 2
Vorschläge zur Leistungsmessung
ISBN 978-3-12-834224-5

5 A special place

Write 6 to 8 sentences about a tourist sight which you know and like. Write about what it is and why you like it, what you can do there, and who else could like this place.

Or:

Look at the notes and the picture and write about the London Eye.

Information:
- on the south side of the Thames, opposite the Houses of Parliament
- ferris wheel[1] is135 m high
- journey[2] time: 30 minutes, wheel doesn't usually stop
- price: £29.95; or £26.96 online

1 **ferris wheel** Riesenrad | 2 **journey** Fahrt

_____

_____

_____

_____

_____

6 Be careful!

▲ *Choose one picture. What's going to happen? Write a dialogue (6 to 8 sentences) where (1) you tell what the man and the woman say **or** (2) what the mother and the Beefeater say to her daughter.*

_____

_____

_____

_____

_____

Green Line 2
Vorschläge zur Leistungsmessung
ISBN 978-3-12-834224-5

7 Queen Elizabeth Olympic Park

You're going to London with your grandparents during a school break, and you're looking for places to visit. Look at the website about Queen Elizabeth Olympic Park and answer their questions.

Tours

The Queen Elizabeth Olympic Park has something for everybody, tourists and Londoners alike[1]. Go on a walking or boat tour and find out about this amazing place. Find out about the 2012 London Olympics and how they improved life here in Stratford (once a poorer[2] part of London with problems but now a popular tourist attraction). Top sportsmen and women used the beautiful buildings first, but now everybody can use the swimming pool and other sports arenas[3].
More …

Food and drink

There are many cafés around the park. Sit outside in summer or inside when it's wet.
More …

How to get here

You can get here easily by train (to Stratford Station or Stratford International), bus (to Stratford Bus Station) or by car (you can park behind Westfields).

What's on?
October

World Cup – Wheelchair tennis
Basketball – London Lions vs. Bristol Flyers
More …

1 **alike** gleichermaßen | 2 **poorer** ärmer | 3 **arena** Stadion

---

Opa: Der Park sieht riesig aus und ich bin nicht so gut zu Fuß. Muss ich überall hinlaufen?

Du: _____

Oma: Und wie kommt man überhaupt hin?

Du: _____

Oma: Stratford – liegt im Osten von London, oder? Was ist das für ein Stadtteil?

Du: _____

Opa: Was kann man dort machen?

Du: _____

Opa: Und gibt es im Oktober, wenn wir da sind, irgendwelche Veranstaltungen dort?

Du: _____

Oma: Und falls es regnet, können wir irgendwo hingehen ohne Sport treiben zu müssen?

Du: _____

© Ernst Klett Verlag GmbH, Stuttgart 2015 | www.klett.de
Von dieser Druckvorlage ist die Vervielfältigung für den eigenen Unterrichtsgebrauch gestattet. Die Kopiergebühren sind abgegolten. Alle Rechte vorbehalten.

Green Line 2
Vorschläge zur Leistungsmessung
ISBN 978-3-12-834224-5

VOCABULARY **8** **Adventure on the Tube ...** → (after Station 1)

Complete the text with the correct words. There are two extra words.

> stop | wheelchair | offered | persuade | change onto | public transport |
> upset | top up | get around | adventure | credit

I remember the first time I used _____ on my own. I went on the Tube!

This is probably an _____ for most people, but even more for me. I can't walk, and

that's why I _____ in a _____. The Tube was so full that

I couldn't get off at my _____ when I needed to! Then a nice woman saw how

_____ I was and she _____ to help me. We got off together, and

she helped me _____ the Central Line so I could get back to where I wanted to go.

Then I needed to _____ my Oyster card for my return journey, but I didn't have

enough money! So she gave me some. I thanked her and sent her the money back the next day.

VOCABULARY **9** **Opposites** → (after Station 2)

Write the opposites.

1. north – _____

2. pro – _____

3. close – _____

4. nobody – _____

5. small – _____

6. to pull – _____

VOCABULARY **10** **The problems of a Beefeater** → (after Station 3)

Fill in the gaps with words from Station 3. You see the first letter of every word.

It's the year 1536 and Charles is one of the king's guards, a B_____, at the Tower

of London. There's an important person in the p_____ at the moment – the

Queen of England. But that's not his job – Charles is the r_____

m_____. An easy job? Not for him. He doesn't like birds and he hates

r_____. When he gives them something to eat, they sometimes

b_____ him. He'd like to have one for dinner, but he can't.

He must be very c_____ with the birds because people believe

that they keep England s_____.

Green Line 2
Vorschläge zur Leistungsmessung
ISBN 978-3-12-834224-5

LANGUAGE **11** **Ready for Mum's birthday party?** → (after Station 1)

Look at the list. What are (✔) or aren't (✗) Luke and his family going to do for Mum's party?
Complete the sentences with the correct form of the going-to future.

clean the house – mum (✗); children (✔)   decorate the house – Jamie and Luke (✔)
go shopping – dad (✔) – children (✗)   cook dinner – dad (✔)
make a cake – Irina and Luke (✔) Jamie (✗)   have a good time – everyone! (✔)
wrap some presents – Jamie and Irina (✔)

Luke's mum _____the house. The children _____ the

house. Dad _____. The children _____ to the

shops with him.

Irina and Luke _____ a cake. Jamie _____

the cake. Jamie and Irina _____ some presents and Jamie and Luke

_____ the house. Dad _____ dinner when he comes

home. They're all _____a good time.

LANGUAGE **12** **Sally asks about Will's weekend plans** → (after Station 1)

Use the words below to write their questions and answers in the going-to future.

1. what – you – do – at the weekend

   _____?

2. we – go – to – London

   _____.

3. you – visit – Buckingham Palace

   _____?

4. no – we – not – visit – any tourist attractions

   _____.

5. why – you – not – do that

   _____?

6. we – watch – a football game

   _____.

Green Line 2
Vorschläge zur Leistungsmessung
ISBN 978-3-12-834224-5

LANGUAGE **13** **Trafalgar Square** → (after Station 1)

Look at the picture and write what is going to happen.

1. A woman _____

_____ .

2. The man _____

_____ .

3. Two children _____

_____ .

4. Two women _____

_____ .

5. A musician _____

_____ .

LANGUAGE **14** **Let's eat something!** → (after Station 2)

The friends are in Greenwich Park. Complete the conversation with **some**, **any**, **every** *or* **no** *or a compound.*

Olivia: I'm really hungry and I've got _____ to eat. I don't really want to go home now.

My sister's friends are there! Has _____ got _____ food to eat?

Dave: No, sorry Olivia. Hey! Let's go _____ to eat. Does _____ want to come?

Luke: Good idea! Where should we go? Do you know _____ new in Greenwich?

Olivia: I know _____ who went to that new pizza place. She said it was good.

Holly: But that's too expensive. I haven't got _____ money. We could go to the café in

the park and get _____ fish and chips. _____ likes that.

Luke: Yes, it's very popular. Look at that queue! The end is _____ close!

Dave: Wait, I know _____ we can go. It costs nothing

and _____ likes the food there. And we can all

eat _____ we like … My house!

Green Line 2
Vorschläge zur Leistungsmessung
ISBN 978-3-12-834224-5

LANGUAGE **15** **Holly at the Tower** → (after Station 3)

Complete the text with the correct adverbs or adjectives.

Holly is visiting the _____ (famous) Tower of London with her mother and her grandparents.

Her grandparents are looking _____ (excited) at everything. It's all new to them. But

Holly is _____ (bored). This isn't her first time here! Then Holly sees a raven. It's sitting

_____ (quiet). She knows that ravens aren't _____ (nervous) birds, but she thinks

there's something wrong with this one. It isn't _____ (happy). There's something wrong with

it." says Holly _____ (sad). "Be _____ (careful)," says her mum _____

(quick), "Ravens can bite _____ (hard)." But the bird doesn't bite Holly. She gives the raven

some bread and the raven eats it _____ (hungry). Holly's grandparents want to go on; they

think the Tower is very _____ (interesting), but Holly wants to stay with the raven. She

gives the bird some water in her hand. It drinks _____ (fast).

A Beefeater is walking _____ (slow) around the Tower when he sees Holly. He walks up

to her and Holly is a little _____ (nervous). But he doesn't look angry! The Beefeater is

_____ (impressed). "Animals know when you like them," he says to Holly.

LANGUAGE **16** **The boys** → (after Station 3)

Compare Luke, Jay and Dave. Fill in the gaps with adverbs in the comparative or superlative form of the underlined word.

1. Luke is a <u>fast</u> runner. Jay is not so fast. → Luke runs _____ than Jay.

2. Dave's friends don't learn things as <u>quickly</u> as Dave does.

   → Dave learns the _____ of all three.

3. Jay is a <u>good</u> singer. Dave can't sing. → Jay sings _____ than Dave.

4. It's <u>easy</u> for Jay to get up in the morning. It isn't easy for Luke!

   → Jay gets up _____ than Luke.

5. Nobody can <u>throw</u> a ball as hard as Luke! → Luke can throw a ball the _____.

6. Jay doesn't work as <u>hard</u> as Dave. → Dave works _____ than Jay.

Green Line 2
Vorschläge zur Leistungsmessung
ISBN 978-3-12-834224-5

VIEWING **17** **A look at the Thames**

a) *Watch the video and write numbers next to the tourist attractions in the order that the speaker talks about them. Be careful! Four attractions aren't in the video.*

☐ Big Ben ☐ The Shard

☐ Buckingham Palace ☐ The Tower of London

☐ The London Eye ☐ The Tower Bridge

☐ London Bridge ☐ Tower Hill

☐ The Houses of Parliament ☐ Thames Barrier

☐ O_2 Arena

b) *Look at the picture of the Thames Barrier above and read the sentences. Are they true or false? Tick ✔ the correct answer.*

	right	wrong
1. This is a bridge.	☐	☐
2. It's a very famous tourist attraction.	☐	☐
3. It keeps London safe from the sea.	☐	☐
4. It's on the east side of London.	☐	☐
5. They built the barrier in 1892.	☐	☐
6. The city used the barrier more than 150 times.	☐	☐

c) *Tick ✔ the correct answer.*

1. The London Eye is …?

a) ☐ next to the Thames b) ☐ next to Big Ben c) ☐ next to the Barrier

2. What is the Shard?

a) ☐ a big bridge b) ☐ a river c) ☐ a tall building

3. How tall is the Shard?

a) ☐ over 200 m b) ☐ over 300m c) ☐ over 400m

4. How many people live in London?

a) ☐ over 1 million b) ☐ over 5 million c) ☐ 8 million

 © Ernst Klett Verlag GmbH, Stuttgart 2015 | www.klett.de
Von dieser Druckvorlage ist die Vervielfältigung für den eigenen Unterrichtsgebrauch
gestattet. Die Kopiergebühren sind abgegolten. Alle Rechte vorbehalten.

Green Line 2
Vorschläge zur Leistungsmessung
ISBN 978-3-12-834224-5

35

Unit 4 Sport is good for you!

1 What's important?

Either:

a) *Listen and tick ✔ the correct answer.*

		true	false
1.	David has just visited Jack at the hospital.	☐	☐
2.	Jack has had an accident and has broken his leg.	☐	☐
3.	A dog bit him in the park.	☐	☐
4.	Jack doesn't play for the TTS football team.	☐	☐
5.	He can't play football for fourteen days.	☐	☐
6.	Thomas Tallis are playing well this year.	☐	☐
7.	Harry thinks the most important thing is to win the match.	☐	☐

▲ **b)** *Listen to the text again and correct the sentences that are wrong.*

_____

_____

_____

_____

_____

Or:

Listen and answer the questions in 1 to 5 words.

1. Why does Jack call David? _____

2. What happened to Jack in the park? _____

3. What can't he do next Saturday? _____

4. Why is David worried? _____

5. How many matches has the Thomas Tallis team won this year? _____

6. How have they played this year? _____

7. What's the most important thing for Harry? _____

Green Line 2
Vorschläge zur Leistungsmessung
ISBN 978-3-12-834224-5

LISTENING **2** A dramatic sea rescue

Either:

a) *Listen to the dialogue. Look at the pictures and the times, and correct the six mistakes.*

It's 2:30 p.m. (2 mistakes)	It's 3 p.m. (1 mistake)	It's 5 p.m. (3 mistakes)

1. _____

2. _____

3. _____

4. _____

5. _____

6. _____

▲ b) *Listen to the dialogue again and answer the questions in 1 to 7 words.*

1. Why was the family in trouble? _____

2 What did Louise Hudson do? _____

3. How did the rescue end? _____

Or:

Read these statements. Then listen to the dialogue. Cross out the words that are wrong and correct them in 1 to 5 words. One of these statements is correct. Which one?

1. Louise Hudson is a radio reporter. _____

2. She talks to Jim Baker on Saturday at 5 p.m. _____

3. She was phoning a friend when she saw that the boat was in trouble. _____

4. The tide was pushing the boat to shore. _____

5. Louise called the lifeboat station. _____

6. The family was cold and scared but not hurt. _____

Green Line 2
Vorschläge zur Leistungsmessung
ISBN 978-3-12-834224-5

3 Running can be dangerous

"Is it OK if I go for a run in the park now, Dad?" Luke asked his dad at 6 o'clock on Thursday evening. "I need to train more for the marathon on Saturday."

"But Luke," his Dad answered, "it's getting dark now, and running in the dark can be dangerous."

"Not if you come with me!" said Luke.

Twenty minutes later, Luke and his dad were running through Greenwich Park. They were chatting and laughing together so they didn't see the young man who was coming towards them. And the young man didn't notice them because he was listening to music on his headphones[1]. Suddenly the man and Mr Elliot ran into each other. "Oh, I'm sorry," said the young man politely.

"No problem," answered Mr Elliot. Then they all went on. But a moment later, Mr Elliot said: "Luke, my phone's gone! That man took it." So they turned round and ran after him. When they finally stopped him, Mr Elliot shouted angrily and grabbed his arm: "Give me the phone!"

The man looked really scared. "OK, OK! Just don't hurt me!" he screamed. Then he threw the phone to Mr Elliot and quickly ran away.

The minute they got home, Luke told his mum everything. Luke was proud of his brave dad.

"What do you mean 'he stole Dad's phone'?" she asked. "Dad's phone is there on the kitchen table!"

1 **headphones** Kopfhörer

Either:

Read the text. Match the sentence parts. Put the matching numbers and letters in the gaps.

1. Luke wants to	a) runs into Mr Elliot.	_____
2 It is getting dark, so his dad	b) is on the kitchen table.	_____
3. While they are in the park, a young man	c) gives them the phone and runs away.	_____
4. A moment later Mr Elliot	d) go for a run in the park.	_____
5. So Luke and Mr Elliot	e) notices that his phone is missing.	_____
6. He's so scared that he	f) run after the man.	_____
7. But it isn't Mr Elliot's phone. His phone	g) goes with him.	_____

Or:

Answer the questions in full sentences.

1. What does Luke want to do on Thursday evening? _____

2. Why does his dad go with him? _____

3. Why don't the young man and Luke and his dad notice each other? _____

_____

4. Why do Luke and his dad run after the man? _____

5. Who has stolen whose phone? _____

© Ernst Klett Verlag GmbH, Stuttgart 2015 | www.klett.de
Von dieser Druckvorlage ist die Vervielfältigung für den eigenen Unterrichtsgebrauch gestattet. Die Kopiergebühren sind abgegolten. Alle Rechte vorbehalten.

Green Line 2
Vorschläge zur Leistungsmessung
ISBN 978-3-12-834224-5

4 The big match!

"I'm sorry, Luke," Mr Jones said on Friday after football training. "You aren't on the team tomorrow. You aren't playing well at the moment. And this match is too important."

I was upset. I wanted to play. I didn't want to be first reserve[1]. But I knew Mr Jones was right. Bolton High had a good team. We needed to win, and I wasn't playing well enough.

The next day the game started slowly. It was clear that both teams were nervous. At half-time[2] the score was 0:0. The crowd was not happy. After 89 minutes there were still no goals. Then somebody shouted, "Hey, Luke, Jack can't play! He's hurt his leg. You're on! Go, go, go!" So there I was suddenly right in the middle of the game. It was the ninetieth minute. Ben Olson had the ball. He was running quickly towards the goal. The goalkeeper[3] came out of the goal. He started running towards Ben. Then suddenly Ben passed the ball to me. There was no time to think. It was now or never. So I kicked the ball as hard as possible. The TTS crowd cheered excitedly. The ball was in the back of the net. Then the match was over and everybody ran onto the pitch. "Hooray!" they all shouted happily. "We've won! Well done[4], Luke!"

1 **first reserve** Ersatzspieler | 2 **half-time** Halbzeit | 3 **goalkeeper** Tormann | 4 **Well done!** Gut gemacht!

Either:

Read the text and complete the sentences in 1 to 7 words.

1. The day before the game, Mr Jones tells Luke _____.

2. When he hears this Luke feels _____.

3. But Luke knows Mr Jones is right because _____.

4. The match starts slowly because _____.

5. A minute before the end of the match the score is _____.

6. Then Luke can play in the game because _____.

7. In the last minute of the game Luke _____.

Or:

Read the text and tick ✔ the correct answer.

	true	false
1. Luke is off the team for the next week.	☐	☐
2. Luke isn't on the team because he doesn't feel well.	☐	☐
3. Not a lot happens in the first 89 minutes of the game.	☐	☐
4. Luke can play after all because Jack has an injury.	☐	☐
5. When the goalkeeper comes out, Luke passes the ball to Ben.	☐	☐
6. The crowd is so excited that they don't make a sound.	☐	☐
7. Luke's team wins in the last minute!	☐	☐

Green Line 2
Vorschläge zur Leistungsmessung
ISBN 978-3-12-834224-5

WRITING **5** **Sports at schools in Germany**

Either:

Write an e-mail to your English e-friend about sports at schools in Germany. Tell him 1) how many sport lessons you have at your school each week, 2) which sports girls/boys usually play, 3) what your favourite sport is and why, 4) if you do sports after school too. Write 6 to 8 sentences.

Dear Daniel,

Thank you for your e-mail and the funny photos you sent me of your Sports Day. They were great! You asked me about PE in Germany. Well, at my school we _____

_____

_____

_____

_____

_____

_____

WRITING **6** **Be careful when you run!**

a) *During the mini marathon one boy fell because of Dave and Jay. Later he went to the doctor. Write the dialogue. There are some words to help you.*

Doctor: Good morning, young man. How can I help you?

Boy: (accident / hurt / leg) _____

Doctor: (how?) _____

Boy: (running / mini marathon / people in animal costumes / fall) _____

_____

Doctor: (walk?) _____

Boy: (hurts) _____

Doctor: (have a look / twist ankle / not broken /prescription / next few days) _____

_____

_____

▲ **b)** *Reading: Running can be dangerous (p. 38): Go on with the dialogue between Luke, his mum and his dad at the end of the story. What are they going to do about the phone?*

Green Line 2
Vorschläge zur Leistungsmessung
ISBN 978-3-12-834224-5

MEDIATION **7** **Children and health**

Vor 100 Jahren haben Kinder sich mehr bewegt[1] als heute. Und sie waren fitter[2]. Damals gab es keinen Fernseher, kein Telefon und kein Internet. Es gab auch keine Autos. Morgens sind die Kinder zur Schule gelaufen, oft lange Strecken. Nachmittags spielten sie meist mit ihren Freunden draußen im Garten, im Park oder auf der Straße. Oder sie arbeiteten auf dem Feld[3]. Sie verbrachten ihre Freizeit nicht mit Fernsehen, im Internet oder mit Videospielen, so wie viele Teenager es heute tun.

1 **sich mehr bewegen** hier: to get more exercise | 2 **fit sein** to be fit (fitter, fittest) | 3 **auf dem Feld arbeiten** to work in the fields

What does this text say about children's health 100 years ago and children's health today? Tell your English friend in six sentences.

_____

_____

_____

_____

_____

_____

_____

MEDIATION **8** **At the doctor's**

While you're on a bike tour in England your father has to go to a doctor. They need your help to understand each other!

Dad: Sage ihm, dass ich gestern einen Fahrradunfall hatte und dass ich mein Bein verletzt habe.

You: _____

 _____

Doctor: Oh I'm sorry! Why didn't you come right away? Have you taken any pills for the pain yet?

You: _____

 _____

Dad: Noch nicht. Könnte er mir bitte ein Rezept für Tabletten und eine Salbe geben?

You: _____

 _____

 _____

Doctor: Of course, but first I'd like to take a careful look at your leg.

You: _____

 _____

Green Line 2
Vorschläge zur Leistungsmessung
ISBN 978-3-12-834224-5

VOCABULARY **9** **Sport verbs** → (after Check-in)

Look at the pictures and write the verbs.

 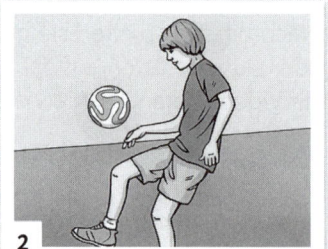 

_____ _____ _____

_____ _____ _____

VOCABULARY **10** **Parts of the body** → (after Station 1)

Look at the picture and write the parts of the body.

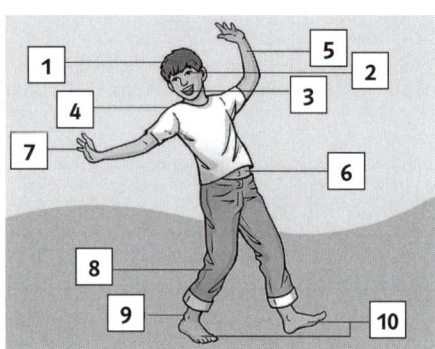

1. _____   6. _____

2. _____   7. _____

3. _____   8. _____

4. _____   9. _____

5. _____   10. _____

VOCABULARY **11** **Saying it differently** → (after Station 2)

Complete the second sentence so that it has the same meaning as the first.

1. Her stomach doesn't feel good! → She feels _____.

2. My head hurts. → I've got _____.

3. Tim's shoulder hurts. → Tim has got a _____ in his shoulder.

4. The doctor wants to see what's wrong with my leg. → He wants to _____ my leg.

5. I've got a bad cold. → I've _____ a bad cold.

6. Lisa's hurt her ankle. → Lisa's _____ her ankle.

 Klett

© Ernst Klett Verlag GmbH, Stuttgart 2015 | www.klett.de
Von dieser Druckvorlage ist die Vervielfältigung für den eigenen Unterrichtsgebrauch
gestattet. Die Kopiergebühren sind abgegolten. Alle Rechte vorbehalten.

Green Line 2
Vorschläge zur Leistungsmessung
ISBN 978-3-12-834224-5

VOCABULARY 12 **Where's Luke?** → (after Station 2)

Holly is on her way to school when she sees Jamie. Complete the dialogue.

Holly: Hi Jamie. Where's Luke?

Jamie: He's in bed. He's c _ _ _ _ _ a bad cold so he can't go to school today.

Holly: Oh no! Has he got a f _ _ _ _ too?

Jamie: No, he hasn't. But he has got a bad c _ _ _ _ and a h _ _ _ _ _ _ _ _ _ !

Oh, and his a _ _ _ hurt and he's even got a p _ _ _ in his l _ _ _ _ !

Holly: Oh no! That doesn't sound good! Has he been to the d _ _ _ _ _ _ y _ _ ?

Jamie: Mum's going to call the Health Centre now so Dr Brown can come and h _ _ _ _

a l _ _ _ _ at him and give him a p _ _ _ _ _ _ _ _ _ _ _ _ _ _ _ .

Holly: Please tell him I hope he feels better soon, OK?

VOCABULARY 13 **Molly's story** → (after Station 3)

Use the words/phrases below to complete Molly's story. There are three extra words/phrases.

| races | award | hurts | almost | trained | yet | cheered | leg | what it's like |
| running | not … yet | cramp | experience | accident |

When I was a three, I lost part of my _____

in an _____. Since[1] then I've worn an

artificial limb[2]. But this hasn't stopped me from

_____! This is something that I love to do,

and I even run in _____ for my school team!

It's been a great _____ for me. Everyone on

my team is very friendly. Sometimes people ask me _____ to wear an artificial limb.

On some days I don't notice it at all – well, _____ not at all – but on others it

_____ a little bit. But it hasn't stopped me _____!

Last year I even won the school sports _____. Everyone _____ for me!

1 **since** seit | 2 **artificial limb** Prothese

Green Line 2
Vorschläge zur Leistungsmessung
ISBN 978-3-12-834224-5

14   Running with the friends   → (after Station 1)

Write questions and short answers. (✔) = yes (✗) = no

Example:

Jay | ever | watch | a marathon? (✔) <u>*Has Jay ever watched a marathon? – Yes, he has.*</u>

1. Luke and Jay | ever | hear of | the mini marathon? (✗)

   _____

2. Dave | ever | run |in a marathon ? (✗)

   _____

3. Luke and his friends |ever | train |in Greenwich Park? (✔)

   _____

4. Olivia |ever | hurt | her ankle before a race? (✔)

   _____

5. Gwen | ever | lose |a race? (✔)

   _____

6. she | ever | win | a marathon? (✗)

   _____

15   An interview with Jim Comber   → (after Station 2)

Jim Comber is the new member of a German football team. Complete the questions and answers.

Reporter: _____ (you – ever – play) outside England?

Comber: Yes, I _____. But I _____ (never – play) in Germany before.

Reporter: _____ (you – meet) your new team yet?

Comber: Yes, I _____. And we _____ (already – do) some training together.

Reporter: _____ (the Tigers – ever – buy) an English player before?

Comber: Yes, they _____. But they _____ (never – pay) so much.

Reporter: _____ (the trainer – give) you any useful tips?

Comber: Yes, and he _____ (already – organise) German lessons

for me too!

Reporter: _____ (you – start) them yet?

Comber: No, I _____.

Green Line 2
Vorschläge zur Leistungsmessung
ISBN 978-3-12-834224-5

A Look at the pictures and talk about them.
What can you see? Would you like to go there?
Why or why not?

A Look at the pictures and talk about them.
What can you see? Would you like to go there?
Why or why not?

AA Look at these two trip brochures.

Explore Outdoor Centre
1 week: £250 with all meals
Activities:
adventure bike riding, swimming, boating, football

Wales Farm
1 week: £125, meals extra
Activities:
hiking, horse riding and cooking lessons; helping with farm animals

Partner A: Everyone wants you and your partner to decide where to go on a class trip.

– *Tell your partner which trip idea you think is best for your class (not just you) and say why.*
– *Listen to your partner's ideas.*
– *Discuss with your partner which idea is best.*

AA Look at these two trip brochures.

Great Fun Outdoor Centre
1 week: £290 with all meals
Activities:
gorge scrambling, mountain climbing, bike riding, forest hikes

Wales Activity Camp
1 week: £180, meals extra
Activities:
mountain walking, visits to towns and museums, tennis, football, dance parties

Partner B: Everyone wants you and your partner to decide where to go on a class trip.

– *Tell your partner which trip idea you think is best for your class (not just you) and say why.*
– *Listen to your partner's ideas.*
– *Discuss with your partner which idea is best.*

This is a picture from last year's yearbook. Describe it. Which club do you think this is? What were the people doing?

You and your partner want to join a club together. Look at all four club pictures and discuss why you like or don't like each club. Find one club that's good for the two of you.

This picture is from last year's yearbook. Describe it. Which club do you think this is? What were the people doing?

You and your partner want to join a club together. Look at all four club pictures and discuss why you like or don't like each club. Find one club that's good for the two of you.

This is a picture from last year's yearbook. Describe it. Which club do you think this is? What were the people doing?

You and your partner want to join a club together. Look at all four club pictures and discuss why you like or don't like each club. Find one club that's good for the two of you.

This is a picture from last year's yearbook. Describe it. Which club do you think this is? What were the people doing?

You and your partner want to join a club together. Look at all four club pictures and discuss why you like or don't like each club. Find one club that's good for the two of you.

B

A

a) *Talk about what you can do and see at these places.*

b) *You can only go to one of the places. Which one do you want to go to and why?*

Buckingham Palace

Hyde Park

a) *Talk about what you can do and see at these places.*

b) *You can only go to one of the places. Which one do you want to go to and why?*

The British Museum

Covent Garden

a) *Imagine you visited all of these places in the pictures last year. Your partner wants to go to one on his / her next holiday (he / she chooses which one). Answer the questions your partner asks you about the place.*

b) *Now swap roles and ask your partner about one of the places in the pictures.*

Buckingham Palace

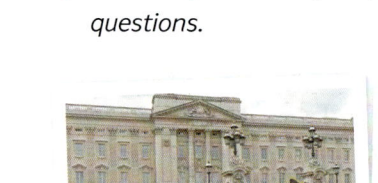

The British Museum

Hyde Park

Covent Garden

a) *Imagine you want to go to one of the places in the pictures on your next holiday. Your partner visited all of them last year. Ask your partner questions about the place that you choose.*

b) *Now swap roles. It's your partner's turn to ask you questions.*

Buckingham Palace

The British Museum

Hyde Park

Covent Garden

Tell the story behind this picture.

Sally White is happy.

After the game, a reporter interviews Sally White for his/her school magazine. Act the dialogue:
Partner A is the reporter and asks Sally 4 questions.
Partner B acts the part of Sally and gives the answers.

Tell the story behind this picture.

Sam Smith is not happy.

A few days after the game, a reporter interviews Sam Smith for his/her school magazine. Act the dialogue:
Partner A is the reporter and asks Sam 4 questions.
Partner B acts the part of Sam and gives the answers.

Tell the story behind this picture.

Lisa Winter is happy.

After the mini marathon, a reporter interviews Lisa Winter for his/her school magazine. Act the dialogue:
Partner A is the reporter and asks Lisa four questions.
Partner B acts the part of Lisa and gives the answers.

Tell the story behind this picture.

John Brown is not happy.

A few days after the mini marathon, a reporter interviews John Brown for his/her school magazine. Act the dialogue:
Partner A is the reporter and asks John four questions.
Partner B acts the part of John and gives the answers.

B

A

B

A

What is happening here? Describe the situation.

 **Partner A:** You (the teacher) see that Karen has a mobile (she isn't allowed to have one in class).
Partner B: You are Karen. You have a mobile, but you know you shouldn't have one in class. Act the role play.

What is happening here? Describe the situation.

 **Partner A:** You're Nick, and all you want to do is play video games.
Partner B: You're Nick's friend and you want him to come outside. You're worried about him.
Act the role play.

What is happening here? Describe the situation.

Partner A: You're the girl who's crying. Tina has sent you a nasty text and you're very upset.
Partner B: You're the friend. Your friend shows you the text from Tina and you try to help her. Act the role play.

What is happening here? Describe the situation.

Partner A: You're Frank (the boy in the picture). You don't know what to do, so you call your friend.
Partner B: You're the friend, and you give Frank advice. Act the role play.

What is happening here? Describe the situation. How do you think it will go on?

 You and your parents were out sightseeing in London and when you get back to the hotel, you have a bad problem! **Partner A** explains the situation to the receptionist (**Partner B**) (Empfangsdame). Act the role play.

What is happening here? Describe the situation. How do you think it will go on?

 You and your parents are on a tour in England. You have a problem and you need to get the bus driver's attention! **Partner A** is the girl and **Partner B** is the father. Act the role play.

What is happening here? Describe the situation. How do you think it will go on?

Your class trip doesn't end well for you! First decide with your partner who the boy is talking to. **Partner A** plays this role. **Partner B** acts the role of the boy. Act the role play.

What is happening here? Describe the situation. How do you think it will go on?

It's awful when you have to say goodbye! What are the friends saying to each other? **Partner A** is the girl with the book and **Partner B** is one of the friends. Act the role play.

B

A

LANGUAGE **16** **Daniel Best** → (after Station 3)

Complete the text with the correct verb forms. Use the present perfect or the simple past.

Daniel Best _____ (already – win) a lot of bike races in Britain. He first _____

(start) racing when he _____ (be) only eight years old. In 2010 he _____ (enter)

his first big competition in England. He _____ (not win) that year, but the experience

_____ (make) him a lot more confident. A year later Daniel _____ (win)

all three races in Britain, but he _____ (not do) well in Austria or in France.

He _____ (not become) one of the world's greatest bike racers yet. But he

_____ (already – earn) a lot of money as one of Britain's most popular sportsmen.

LANGUAGE **17** **Before school** → (after Station 3)

It's 8:30 a.m. and Dave is still at home. Complete the dialogue with the correct verb forms. Use the present perfect or the simple past.

Mum: _____ (finish) your

breakfast yet, Dave?

Dave: Yes, I _____, Mum, and I_____

(already – put) everything into my schoolbag.

Mum: Well, what about these running shoes? I _____ (just – find)

them under your bed. Don't you need them for PE today?

Dave: No, Mum! Our PE lesson _____ (be) yesterday.

Mum: Oh! _____ (take) them to school with you yesterday?

Dave: No, I _____. I _____ (forget). But I _____ (not

need) them anyway because Mr Winton _____ (not be) at school yesterday.

Mum: So you _____ (not have) a PE lesson?

Dave: Yes, we _____. But we _____ (do) judo with Mr Wallace.

Mum: That _____ (be) lucky for you! Well, are you sure you've got everything you

need for today?

Dave: Yes, Mum. I'm sure I _____ (forget) anything today.

Green Line 2
Vorschläge zur Leistungsmessung
ISBN 978-3-12-834224-5

Unit 5 Stay in touch

LISTENING **1 Talking about advice**

Either:

Listen to Holly and Olivia's conversation. Which of the sentences below are about John, Filip or Steve? Tick ✔ one correct answer.

	John	Filip	Steve
1. He thinks he must come home earlier at weekends than everyone else.	☐	☐	☐
2. His friends are upset but he doesn't know why.	☐	☐	☐
3. He wants something because it's newer.	☐	☐	☐
4. Ruby says it's right that his friends are angry with him.	☐	☐	☐
5. Ruby thinks maybe there could be different rules for special events.	☐	☐	☐
6. Olivia and Holly are in the same situation as he is, so they want to talk to their parents too.	☐	☐	☐
7. Olivia has the same problem he does, but she's not upset about it.	☐	☐	☐

Or:

a) *Listen and tick ✔ the correct answer.*

	true	false
1. John posted photos of his friends on a school trip.	☐	☐
2. John's friends aren't happy.	☐	☐
3. Ruby thinks John's friends are wrong.	☐	☐
4. Filip wants to stay out later on school nights.	☐	☐
5. Holly can't stay out later than Filip, but Olivia can.	☐	☐
6. Ruby thinks different rules can be possible for special events.	☐	☐
7. Steve wants a new smartphone because his is old.	☐	☐
8. Ruby thinks a smartphone isn't a good idea for a present for Steve.	☐	☐

▲ **b)** *Listen again and correct the wrong sentences.*

Green Line 2
Vorschläge zur Leistungsmessung
ISBN 978-3-12-834224-5

LISTENING **2** **A school project**

Either:

a) *Listen and put the correct pictures in the right order. Two pictures don't show what happened during Henry's week!*

▲ **b)** *Explain why the two pictures are wrong. Write sentences below.*

1. _____

2. _____

Or:

Listen and complete the sentences with 1 to 7 words.

1. His mother helped Henry with his project when she _____.

2. He was afraid that his friends _____.

3. But it got easier and he even had more conversations with _____.

4. Henry and his friends had to talk _____.

5. They weren't allowed to use social media, but they still _____.

6. Henry still wants his smartphone because this is how _____.

7. Now he still wants to use his smartphone, but _____.

Green Line 2
Vorschläge zur Leistungsmessung
ISBN 978-3-12-834224-5

3 Stay safe online!

A Don't post any personal information online – like your address, e-mail address or mobile number – and don't tell anyone[1] your real name, the school you go or the sports team or clubs you belong to.

B When you've put a picture of yourself online, most people can see it and download it, it's not just yours any more. Be careful what you post about yourself or others – or let your friends post about you – because you may have to live with it for many years.

C Don't give your username or password to anyone. If someone logs on and says they are you, everyone thinks it *is* you! They can write all kinds of awful things – and then you have a problem!

D Don't be friends with people you don't know. If someone online makes you feel worried: Leave the website, turn off your computer and talk to your parents or teacher.

E Remember that not everyone online is who they say they are. If you don't know them, they aren't your friend and you don't need them – you have lots of *real* friends!

F Don't be rude or write 'hate mail'. Maybe you don't like what someone has said – so just block the message. You can't hide[2] behind your computer – someone knows what you're writing!

1 **don't tell anyone** sag nicht jedem | 2 **hide** sich verstecken

Either:

Read the text. Which headings and text parts go together? Put a letter next to each heading.
There is one extra heading.

1. Upset by what's online? – ask for help! _____

2. Don't give someone bad the chance to be you! _____

3. Real friends are outside your computer! _____

4. Find out which social network is safe! _____

5. Keep your identity safe online! _____

6. Be careful – people know if you've been nasty! _____

7. Online you have an audience for long time! _____

Or:

a) *Read the text and tick ✔ the correct answer.*

	true	false	line number(s)
1. Tell someone if you're upset about something online.	☐	☐	
2. Be as nasty as you like in your e-mails – it's no problem!	☐	☐	
3. The pictures you post stay online for a long time.	☐	☐	
4. It's OK to tell everybody online where you go in your free time.	☐	☐	
5. Online friends are the best kind of friends.	☐	☐	
6. People can use your password to make trouble.	☐	☐	

▲ **b)** *Give the line numbers where you found your answers.*

c) *Correct the wrong sentences.*

Green Line 2
Vorschläge zur Leistungsmessung
ISBN 978-3-12-834224-5

READING **4** **Keeping in touch**

Holly gets an e-mail from Emily, a friend who has moved to another town and goes to a new school.

> Hi Holly! My new school is really big – you have to walk a long way to get to each classroom. Before school the first day everyone was talking and no one said hello. I was alone! When a few people noticed me, they stared and whispered! It was so embarrassing! I didn't just want to stand there, but I didn't know what to do. Then in the first lesson the teacher introduced me, and lots of people wanted to know all about me! From then on things went better.
> Before I moved here my cousin said I shouldn't talk about myself too much, but it was difficult because everyone asked me questions! His other advice was to pay attention[1] in lessons because teachers always notice new students. So, I've been working hard, but not too hard – nobody likes the teacher's favourite! This week I've joined the Drama Club. I think clubs are the best way to make new friends – you all enjoy the same activity, so you have a lot to talk about. I really miss you all! I hope you haven't forgotten me! Write soon!. Love, Emily.

1 **pay attention** aufpassen

Either:

Read the text and choose the correct answer(s). More than one answer can be correct.

1. The classrooms at the new school are …

   a) ☐ easy to find.

   b) ☐ far from each other.

   c) ☐ old.

2. Before school started, …

   a) ☐ Emily said hello to everyone.

   b) ☐ nobody noticed Emily.

   c) ☐ Emily wanted something to do.

3. Before the first lesson Emily felt …

   a) ☐ lonely.

   b) ☐ relaxed.

   c) ☐ embarrassed.

4. When she was finally in class, Emily …

   a) ☐ talked about herself *(sich selbst)*.

   b) ☐ followed part of her cousin's advice.

   c) ☐ asked a lot of questions.

5. During her lessons Emily …

   a) ☐ works as much as she can.

   b) ☐ works enough, but not too much.

   c) ☐ doesn't do her work.

6. Emily thinks you meet people in clubs …

   a) ☐ who can become your friends.

   b) ☐ who want to do different things.

   c) ☐ who like the same things as you.

Or:

Complete the sentences with the correct answers. Each answer has 1 to 6 words.

1. First Emily felt _____ and _____ and the others _____ and _____ .

2. But after the teacher introduced her in class _____ .

3. She didn't follow all of her cousin's advice because _____

   _____ and she didn't want to be the teacher's favourite.

4. When you join a club you can make friends because _____ .

Green Line 2
Vorschläge zur Leistungsmessung
ISBN 978-3-12-834224-5

5 I want a party!

You've received this e-mail from your friend Ben.

> Hi!
>
> How was your school trip to the Technology Museum yesterday? Good, I hope.
>
> I need to ask you for some advice. You know it's my birthday next month? Well, Mum and Dad want the whole family to go away for a weekend by the sea – on the weekend of my birthday! My brother and sister are really excited about it, but I don't want to go – I really want to have a party at home. I'm not allowed to stay at home alone, so I have to go with them.
>
> Mum says I should be happy to celebrate with the family, but I want to celebrate with my friends. I don't know what to do! I'd really like your advice.
>
> Ben

Write an e-mail to Ben. Remember to use useful phrases for giving advice.

- begin with a greeting
- say that you enjoyed your school trip. Why?
- show that you understand how he feels
- give some advice
- finish your e-mail

_____

_____

_____

_____

_____

_____

WRITING **6** Agony aunt contest

▲ *There's an agony aunt contest in your English class. First, think of a situation (or use one of the ideas below) and then write the advice letter for it. Be as creative as you can!*

- Person A wants to ask Person B to a party. Person A is very shy and doesn't know what to say.
- Suddenly your friend acts like he/she hates you, and you don't know why.
- Someone wants to use a social network, but his/her parents don't allow it.

_____

_____

_____

_____

Green Line 2
Vorschläge zur Leistungsmessung
ISBN 978-3-12-834224-5

7 Advice about different interests

Your English pen pal Kevin is visiting you. Both of you are at home and are watching TV. Your little brother Tom comes in and looks upset. Kevin wants to help Tom, but his German isn't good and your brother's English isn't good. Help them talk to each other.

Kevin: Hi Tom! Uh, what's the matter! You look really sad!

You: _____

_____

Tom: Meine Freunde wollen in ihrer Freizeit nur Sport machen!
Ich bin nicht gut in Sport und es macht mir nicht viel Spaß. Ich weiß nicht, was ich tun soll!

You: _____

_____

_____

Kevin: Have you tried talking to them about it? Maybe you can find a compromise! Why don't you try to have fun together in other ways? You could go to a film or play video games …

You: _____

_____

_____

Tom: Ich kann sie nicht dazu bringen etwas zu machen, was sie nicht machen wollen!

You: _____

Kevin: But you can't know what they're going to say when you haven't asked them yet! The next step is to call them, or if you're too nervous, why don't you text them?

You: _____

_____

_____

Tom: Ich hoffe, dass sie nicht denken, dass ich blöd bin, aber ich werde es trotzdem versuchen.

You: _____

_____

Green Line 2
Vorschläge zur Leistungsmessung
ISBN 978-3-12-834224-5

8 **Media collocations** → (after Station 1)

Match the verbs with the correct nouns to make the correct media collocations. Put the letters next to the verbs. Sometimes there can be two answers.

1. to change _____   a) a forum
2. to join _____   b) information
3. to stay in touch with _____   c) a discussion
4. to take part in _____   d) photos
5. to post _____   e) an e-mail
6. to share _____   f) your profile
7. to chat with _____   g) a friend
8. to reply to _____   h) a message

9 **What should you do?** → (after Station 2)

You're an agony aunt and people call you and ask for advice. Do you know what to do? Which answer(s) should you give for each situation? Sometimes two are possible!

1. While your caller tells you a problem, it's a good idea for you to …

   a) ☐ act like you don't care. b) ☐ show your understanding. c) ☐ listen carefully.

2. It doesn't help your caller if you are …

   a) ☐ interested.   b) ☐ fair.   c) ☐ nasty.

3. When you want to ask what your caller has tried, you can start your question with …

   a) ☐ Why don't you …?   b) ☐ Have you tried …   c) ☐ What on earth …?

4. Your caller is having a fight with a friend. It may be a good idea for the caller to …

   a) ☐ find a compromise.   b) ☐ overreact.   c) ☐ forgive the friend.

5. Your caller thinks he/she is always right and his/her friend is wrong. The caller should …

   a) ☐ be more self-critical.   b) ☐ say the friendship is over.   c) ☐ say he/she is always right.

6. Is your caller very upset with you? Then tell him/her to …

   a) ☐ worry.   b) ☐ hang up.   c) ☐ calm down.

7. Your caller is upset about what was in a friend's e-mails. It may be good for the two of them to …

   a) ☐ talk face-to-face.   b) ☐ block their e-mails.   c) go crazy.

8. Your caller feels nervous about a chat room he/she has visited. He/She should …

   a) ☐ relax.   b) ☐ stay away from it.   c) ☐ tell an adult about it.

Klett
© Ernst Klett Verlag GmbH, Stuttgart 2015 | www.klett.de
Von dieser Druckvorlage ist die Vervielfältigung für den eigenen Unterrichtsgebrauch
gestattet. Die Kopiergebühren sind abgegolten. Alle Rechte vorbehalten.

Green Line 2
Vorschläge zur Leistungsmessung
ISBN 978-3-12-834224-5

LANGUAGE **10** **Ideas that changed the world!** → (after Station 1)

*Use **after, before, as soon as, until, whenever, like, because** or **when** to complete Terry's e-mail.*
Sometimes there's more than one answer, but you only need to give one.

Hi Peter! The visit to the Communication and Technology Museum was great! A few

minutes _____ we arrived, a guide gave us an interesting description of the

four parts of the museum: the phone, the radio, the TV, the internet. I think this is a great

museum _____ you can touch[1] things and watch short films that explain them.

_____ we touched a screen[2], we saw actors who were acting _____

they were watching TV or using a phone for the first time. We couldn't leave _____

we tried using the very old telephones – I went into another room and my friend Bill phoned

me. It sounded _____ he was *very* far away when he spoke! I had to wait a while

_____ I could answer. Write soon. Dave.

1 **to touch** anfassen | 2 **screen** Bildschirm

LANGUAGE **11** **Project time** → (after Station 1)

Complete the dialogue with question tags.

Mr Green: Listen please, everyone. You remember I spoke to you last

week about your next Technology project, _____?

I need your ideas tomorrow, please.

Holly: We can send you our ideas by e-mail, _____?

Mr Green: Yes, that's fine. I just want to check that your ideas are OK before you start your work.

Holly: You've said there's lots of time to do everything, _____?

Luke: We don't have to finish it until Friday, _____?

Mr Green: Well, I can't give you *a lot* of time! You haven't got any projects at the moment for your

other teachers, _____? But I'm a nice teacher, _____? Give me your

ideas tomorrow. Next Wednesday the projects must be finished.

Olivia: Holly and I spoke yesterday about our ideas, _____, Holly?

Holly: Yes – we've got a *great* idea! I'm going to e-mail it to you this evening, Mr Green.

(whispering) Olivia, he's never given us so much time before, _____?

Green Line 2
Vorschläge zur Leistungsmessung
ISBN 978-3-12-834224-5

LANGUAGE **12**

Gwen's life at home → (after Station 2)

Complete the text with the correct substitute forms in the simple present ((not) allowed to, (not) able to, (not) have to). Use short forms if you can.

I'm good at music so I _____ help my sister to learn to play the saxophone.

As you know, I _____ see very well, but when my sister helps me, we

_____ go to lots of places together. We _____ stay out after

8 o'clock on school nights, but on Fridays and Saturdays we _____ stay at our

friends' houses until much later. My mum doesn't think I can help her in the kitchen because I she thinks

I _____ find things easily – it's not really true, but I _____

tell her that, do I? I don't like everything she cooks for us, but I love it when she says I

_____ choose my favourite meal – pizza!

LANGUAGE **13**

When my dad was young ... → (after Station 2)

Complete the text with the correct substitute forms in the simple past. Use short forms if you can.

Yesterday my dad told me about how different life was when he was as old as I am now. Of course,

he and his friends didn't have mobile phones, so whenever they were out of the house,

they _____ call each other and decide

where to meet – they _____ go home to

use the phone! He said he _____ watch

TV only for an hour every evening – and they didn't have the

internet then, so he _____ play video

games or chat online. That sounds boring to me, but he said

because of this he _____ spend more time with his friends face-to-face than I do

with mine. He _____ do after-school activities because his school was far from

home, and there wasn't a school bus later in the afternoon. He _____ help around

the house when he got home on school days because he _____ do homework, and

he _____ do anything else until this was finished.

Klett

© Ernst Klett Verlag GmbH, Stuttgart 2015 | www.klett.de
Von dieser Druckvorlage ist die Vervielfältigung für den eigenen Unterrichtsgebrauch
gestattet. Die Kopiergebühren sind abgegolten. Alle Rechte vorbehalten.

Green Line 2
Vorschläge zur Leistungsmessung
ISBN 978-3-12-834224-5

LANGUAGE **14**   **Giving advice**   → (after Station 2)

*Give advice for the problems. Write sentences with **should**, **shouldn't** or **could** and the ideas below.*

1. I always forget my friends' birthdays. It's embarrassing! (write them in your planner)

   _____

2. I want to learn more about people from the past. (read history books or go to a history museum)

   _____

3. I like to sing and dance. Which clubs are there for me? (take part in the Music or Dance Club)

   _____

4. I told one friend another friend's secret and now he's angry with me. (not pass on secrets)

   _____

5. I fell yesterday and my leg still hurts. (go to the doctor)

   _____

6. I think I'm always wrong. What should do? (not to be too self-critical)

   _____

LANGUAGE **15**   **Looking for advice**   → (after Station 2)

▲ *Complete each gap with either a modal or a substitute form.*

Dear Ruby, my parents are worried that I play video games too much. They

say that I _____ get out of my bedroom more! And they say

I _____ do a lot of things really well, like sport and music, so they _____

understand why I don't spend more time doing them. They make me feel really bad! I'm always telling

them that I work *very* hard at school, so I _____ relax sometimes! And video games are

my favourite hobby. I do a lot of sport at school, so I _____ do more in my free time! Also,

I really don't enjoy playing my saxophone any more because when I was younger, I _____

practise every day. I _____ stay in my room and play video games then, so I'm going to

do it now and they _____ try and stop me. My brother _____ do what he

wanted in his free time when he was as old as I am now. He _____ play sport or music,

so I don't know why they're trying to make *me* do it! What _____ I do?

Green Line 2
Vorschläge zur Leistungsmessung
ISBN 978-3-12-834224-5

Unit 6 Goodbye Greenwich

LISTENING **1** **A family trip**

Either:

Listen. Mary and her father, mother and her little sister Sally are talking about their next trip. What do they say you can do at these different places? Write the letters next to the correct places.

Place	Letter (A–H)	Activities
Cornwall		**A.** Visit the Festival
		B. Go to a living history show
Ireland		**C.** Enjoy the fantastic Welsh landscape
		D. Go on a pony trekking tour
		E. Visit lots of museums and theatres
Edinburgh		**F.** Relax under palm trees
		G. Go on a hiking tour
Cardiff		**H.** Eat fish and chips

Or:

Listen. Mary and her father, mother and her little sister Sally are talking about their next trip. Tick ✔ the correct answers. There can be more than one correct answer.

1. Her father wants to go to a beach in…

   a) ☐ England.

   b) ☐ Ireland.

   c) ☐ Wales.

2. Her mother says they can …

   a) ☐ go to Edinburgh.

   b) ☐ go to Dublin.

   c) ☐ go pony trekking.

3. Her father doesn't want to go to Edinburgh …

   a) ☐ because there is no festival at that time.

   b) ☐ because it will cost too much money.

   c) ☐ because he doesn't like the city.

4. Mary first found out about Cardiff from …

   a) ☐ the internet.

   b) ☐ a friend's mum.

   c) ☐ her teacher.

5. Mary thinks Cardiff is a good idea because …

   a) ☐ there are lots of tours and culture there.

   b) ☐ they can visit a medieval castle.

   c) ☐ they don't have to go to a boring beach.

6. When her father hears Mary's idea, he …

   a) ☐ wants to find a different idea.

   b) ☐ wants to get more information.

   c) ☐ still wants to go to Cornwall.

Green Line 2
Vorschläge zur Leistungsmessung
ISBN 978-3-12-834224-5

LISTENING **2** **The Newcastle Morning Show**

Either:

Listen to the weather forecast and complete the sentences in 1 to 7 words.

1. It's a good idea to be outside on Saturday

   because _____ .

2. There will be a weather change on _____ .

3. You'll want to stay inside because _____ .

4. You can learn a lot about Newcastle's history if you take a tour of one of its _____ .

5. If you must be outside on Sunday, it's better to wait till _____ .

6. You won't be able to see the stars at night because _____ .

7. You'll be able to see the stars better _____ .

Or:

a) *Listen to the weather forecast. Which phrases describe what the weather will be like on Saturday and Sunday? Write the correct letters below each day. Be careful! There's one extra letter!*

a) cloudy later in the day
b) warm and sunny
c) storms in the morning
d) lots of rain and wind
e) high of 18 degrees (Grad)
f) a good night to see the stars

g) great weather all day
h) better weather in the afternoon
i) high of 24 degrees
j) great day for a walk
k) a good day to stay inside

Saturday:	Sunday:

b) *Listen again and tick* ✔ *the correct answer.*

	true	false
1. It'll be a great start to the weekend to take a walk along Hadrian's Wall.	☐	☐
2. There will be storms and rain and wind on Saturday night.	☐	☐
3. If you aren't careful, you'll get wet outside on Sunday!	☐	☐
4. You can learn about how Victoria was in the past in the Newcastle Tunnel.	☐	☐
5. It will be warmer on Sunday than on Saturday.	☐	☐
6. Star watchers can go to bed early on Sunday night.	☐	☐

▲ **c)** *Correct the wrong sentences.*

Green Line 2
Vorschläge zur Leistungsmessung
ISBN 978-3-12-834224-5

57

3 **Moving house for a year**

Read Terry's e-mail to Tim about his news.

> Hey Tim, I still can't believe it. My dad has to go to New York for a year for his job, and we have to go with him. We still have four months before we leave, but Mum is already panicking. What should we do with Bobby (would you like a dog while we're gone?), what should we put in our suitcases (only one for each of us)? She started her lists the minute Dad told her. And my sister is writing lists too, not for what she wants to take there, but for all the clothes she'll buy in New York and bring back here! And my dad is always running around and singing New York songs – I've never seen him so excited before! I didn't even know he could sing! What about me? I'll miss our class trip, our parties, our crazy weekends – and most of all I'll miss you. It's not fair! Dad and Mum say if I try to be positive, I'll find things to look forward to. And I guess it will be exciting to live in a city as famous as New York. I've chatted with a boy who goes to the school I'll go to. His dad works with my dad, and they've been in New York for two months. He says it's cool and he doesn't miss home at all. I'm sure I'll never say that, but maybe it'll be an adventure! I'll write more soon! Terry

Either:

How do they feel because of the move to New York? Give examples from the text that show this.

Person	How does he/she feel?	Examples from the text
mum		
sister		
dad		
Terry		

Or:

Read the text and tick ✔ the correct answers. There can be more than one correct answer.

1. Terry's dad will go to New York because …
   - a) ☐ he lost his old job.
   - b) ☐ he'll work for someone different.
   - c) ☐ he'll do the same job, but in New York.

2. Bobby is …
   - a) ☐ Terry's brother.
   - b) ☐ Terry's friend.
   - c) ☐ Terry's pet.

3. How does Mum feel?
   - a) ☐ unhappy
   - b) ☐ nervous
   - c) ☐ excited

4. Terry's sister is writing lists about…
   - a) ☐ what she'll bring to New York.
   - b) ☐ the fashion she'll see in New York.
   - c) ☐ what she wants to buy in New York.

5. What surprises Terry about his dad?
   - a) ☐ that his dad can sing
   - b) ☐ that his dad got a new job
   - c) ☐ that his dad is so excited

6. Which best describes how Terry feels?
   - a) ☐ sad and angry
   - b) ☐ upset but maybe a little excited
   - c) ☐ happy but a little nervous

© Ernst Klett Verlag GmbH, Stuttgart 2015 | www.klett.de
Von dieser Druckvorlage ist die Vervielfältigung für den eigenen Unterrichtsgebrauch gestattet. Die Kopiergebühren sind abgegolten. Alle Rechte vorbehalten.

Green Line 2
Vorschläge zur Leistungsmessung
ISBN 978-3-12-834224-5

4 **Travel, but carefully!**

Luke finds this article in a travel magazine:

We travel to have fun in new places, to discover animal and plant life, or to learn about the art and culture of different cities. On the one hand, there's nothing wrong with this. We can have exciting experiences and get to know new people and enjoy new things.

But on the other hand, travel can cause serious problems. For example, there's pollution, big hotels that block coastlines, animals and plants that lose the environments where they live, money that sometimes goes to the big tourist businesses[1] and not to the local people who really need it.

So what can you do? Lots! For example, think carefully about how you move through the world. Flying[2] causes a lot of pollution, so take the train or the bus. Use public transport. If you can, book your room at a smaller hotel that belongs to local people. Don't waste electricity or water. Buy from local businesses. Throw away what you don't need in the right way and don't just drop it somewhere (even if you see local people who do this)! Maybe recycling is even possible!

There isn't one solution for the problems, but there are things we can do to travel more carefully.

1 **business** Geschäft | 2 **flying** Fliegen

Either:

Read the text. Put the letter of each of the ideas from the text in the correct group below.

a) meet new people
b) stay at local people's hotels
c) use buses and trains
d) try exciting and new things
e) animals and plants lose their homes
f) don't use too much water and electricity
g) learn about other cultures and art
h) it can cause pollution
i) tourist money often doesn't go to local people
j) throw something away in the right place
k) buy from local shops
l) recycling
m) coastlines are full of hotels
n) discover new plants and animals

Good things about travel	Bad things about travel	Possible solutions

Or:

a) *Which of these peoples' statements match the ideas in the text? Tick ✔ the ones that match.*

1. "I travel to have fun and I don't want to think about bad results my trip can cause!" ☐

2. "It's not possible to travel in a way that's OK for the environment, so I stay at home." ☐

3. "I can help local people when I stay at their hotels and buy things in their shops." ☐

4. "It's better for my trip to start at the train or bus station and not at the airport!" ☐

5. "Even when I'm not at home, I always turn off lights and take short showers!" ☐

6. "Think about how I throw things away when I'm travelling? That's too much trouble!" ☐

▲ **b)** *Explain why some of the statements don't match the ideas in the text.*

Green Line 2
Vorschläge zur Leistungsmessung
ISBN 978-3-12-834224-5

WRITING **5** Holidays in England or Wales

*Imagine you're on holiday for a week in **one** of the following places. Choose one of the places and then write a postcard (6 to 8 sentences) to your English pen friend. Tell him/her about …*

the places you've visited | the activities you've already done | another thing you're going to do |
the weather | the people | when you'll be back home

Cornwall   **Wales**   **London**

_____

_____

_____

_____

_____

_____

WRITING **6** What will / won't my life be like in 2030?

Write six sentences about what your life will or won't be like in 2030. You can use four of the ideas here, but you need to think of two more ideas of your own.

_____

_____

_____

_____

_____

Green Line 2
Vorschläge zur Leistungsmessung
ISBN 978-3-12-834224-5

7 **Travelling by train**

You're at a train station in London and you meet two German tourists and their two children. They don't understand the train information and they need your help. Read the tourists' questions and use the timetable to answer them.

TIMETABLE / TICKET FARES
London Euston – Liverpool Lime Street (change trains at Crewe)

	departure	arrival	departure	arrival	departure	arrival
Euston	3:10 p.m.		3:40 p.m.		4:10 p.m.	
Crewe		4:47 p.m.		5:10 p.m.		5:47 p.m.
Crewe	4:57 p.m.		5:32 p.m.		5:57 p.m.	
Liverpool		5:45 p.m.		6:11 p.m.		6:44 p.m.

TICKET FARES
Adults: single £154.50   return £309   **Children**:   single £77   return £154.50

Tourist: Wir müssen ganz schnell nach Liverpool. Wann fährt der nächste Zug?

Du: _____

Tourist: Oje! Wir müssen noch Fahrkarten kaufen. Welche späteren Verbindungen gibt es denn?

Du: _____

Tourist: Müssen wir umsteigen? Wenn ja, wann fährt der Zug weiter?

Du: _____

Tourist: In Ordnung. Und wie lange brauchen wir dann noch bis Liverpool?

Du: _____

Tourist: Wie viel kosten die Tickets für zwei Erwachsene für die Hin- und Rückfahrt?

Du: _____

Tourist: Und was kostet das für beide Kinder?

Du: _____

Tourist: Vielen Dank!

Green Line 2
Vorschläge zur Leistungsmessung
ISBN 978-3-12-834224-5

8 **Another trip by train**

You're in London with your parents on holiday. You're at the London Waterloo station, and you need to buy some tickets for your train trip to Liverpool. You speak English better than your parents, so you talk to the man at the ticket centre. Remember to be polite!

Man: Good afternoon. How may I help you?

Papa: Frag ihn bitte, wann der nächste Zug nach Liverpool abfährt.

Du: _____

Man: That's at 3:10 p.m. The train gets to Liverpool at 5:45 p.m.

Du: _____

Papa: Aber wir müssen etwas essen bevor wir einsteigen. Welche späteren Verbindungen gibt es denn? Aber ich möchte, dass wir vor 7 Uhr abends in Liverpool ankommen!

Du: _____

Man: There are also trains at 3:40 p.m. and at 4:10 p.m. The train at 4:10 gets to Liverpool at 6:44 p.m.

Du: _____

Mum: Muss man umsteigen bei der Verbindung um 4:10?

Du: _____

Man: Yes, you'll need to once.

Du: _____

Mum: Und wie viel kosten die Tickets für die Hin- und Rückfahrt?

Du: _____

Man: They cost £309 for adults and £154.50 for children older than five.

Du: _____

Papa: Sind die Tickets immer so teuer?

Du: _____

Man: The tickets are cheaper if you book them early, or if you can travel on different days and at different times.

Du: _____

Du (bedankst dich für seine Hilfe): _____

Green Line 2
Vorschläge zur Leistungsmessung
ISBN 978-3-12-834224-5

VOCABULARY **9** **Places and what you can do there** (after Check-in)

For each picture, write down which place this is and three activities you can do there.

place: _____   place: _____   place: _____

_____   _____   _____

_____   _____   _____

_____   _____   _____

VOCABULARY **10** **Weather words** (after Station 1)

What will the weather be like today? Look at the pictures and finish the sentences.

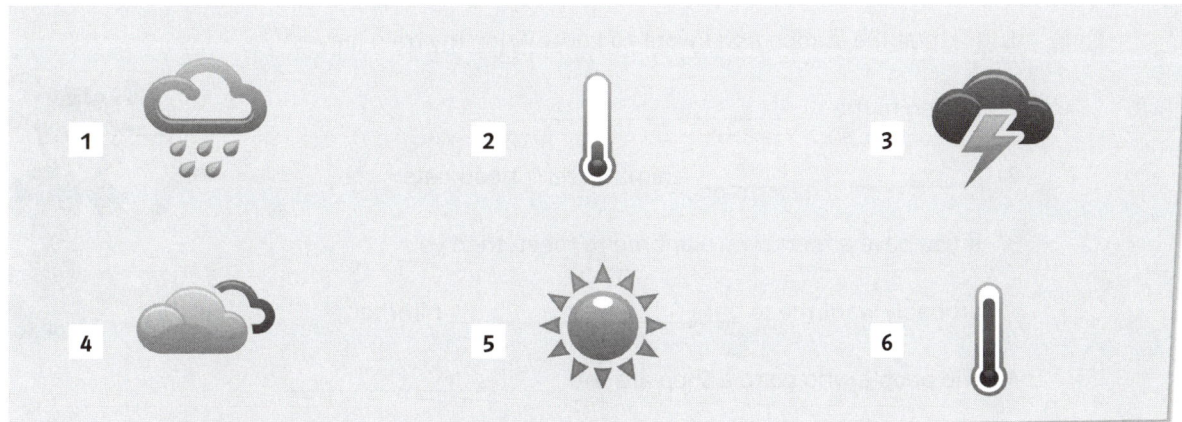

1. Good morning! Our day will start with _____.

2. Don't wear your shorts yet, because it's _____ for a summer morning!

3. Be careful! In some places there will be storms with _____.

4. The weather will be better during your lunch break, but there will still be _____

   above us.

5. Later in the afternoon it will be clear and we'll have a good chance to see the _____.

6. Now is the time for the T-shirts and shorts! At 28°C, it will feel more like summer because it will be

   nice and _____.

Green Line 2
Vorschläge zur Leistungsmessung
ISBN 978-3-12-834224-5

 Klett

VOCABULARY **11** **A weekend trip** (after Station 1)

Read the text and fill in the missing words. All the missing words are from station 1!

A lot of people like to take short trips over the weekend. Before they _____ their tickets,

they get more information on the internet or at a _____. Will they go by bus or by train?

This decision usually _____ a lot of things. First, what is the price of the tickets? Then,

who has the best connection (it's no fun when you have to _____ buses or trains a lot).

And travel times are also important: When does the bus or train _____ and when does

it_____? What kind of ticket do they need? A single ticket or a _____

ticket? How much do tickets cost? Is there a special _____ for groups? This means the

price of the ticket _____ person can be cheaper.

VOCABULARY **12** **Guess the word!** (after Station 2)

Can you guess the words Tony is describing for you? They're all from Station 2!

1. If I'm at the station and I want to know when my train leaves,

   I listen to the _____.

2. _____ animals aren't good pets.

3. If you have a friend you want me to meet, then you

   probably want me to _____ him/her.

4. The people who go to a shop are the _____.

5. In our town there are _____ that help us to remember historical events.

6. The part of the land that is next to the sea is the _____.

7. People in your town are from many different countries, or they are _____.

8. Karl has been living in England for many years, but he still has a German _____.

9. The people from Ireland are the _____.

10. You see a _____ in a church.

Green Line 2
Vorschläge zur Leistungsmessung
ISBN 978-3-12-834224-5

LANGUAGE **13** **The friends' weekend trip to Cornwall** (after Station 1)

Dave's friends want to visit him. Olivia has read the weather forecast, and they are talking about what to bring. Use the will future to complete the conversation. Use short forms if possible.

Olivia: We _____ (have) sun on both days and it _____ (not rain) at all!

Jay: Cool. But what clothes _____ you _____ (bring) for the weekend?

Olivia: It _____ (be) warm, so leave your cold weather clothes at home!

Holly: I _____ (take) some T-shirts and a pair of short trousers. And you, Olivia?

Olivia: Oh I don't know. I need new clothes for the summer, and I think I _____ (go)

shopping this afternoon. _____ you both _____ (come) with me?

Jay: That's a good idea. I _____ (buy) new clothes and some food for the trip too.

Holly: I _____ (not be able) to go with you. I promised Mum I'll be home early.

LANGUAGE **14** **What they do in different situations** (after Station 2)

*The pictures show what people **can/will/should do** in these situations. Complete the sentences.*

1. If it rains, _____

2. If they go to the lake, _____

3. _____ if he runs fast enough!

4. If you feel tired, _____

5. If you see someone who has had an accident,_____

6. _____ if you go to that restaurant!

Green Line 2
Vorschläge zur Leistungsmessung
ISBN 978-3-12-834224-5

LANGUAGE **15** **A trip to London** (after Station 2)

a) *A travel agent is telling you about London. Write sentences with **if + will/can/should** or the **imperative** and the word tips. You can start with the if-clause or the main clause, but remember when you need commas!*

1. (will) have a good time / go to London

   _____

2. (should) want to go in the summer / book trip early

   _____

3. (can) not into tours / go everywhere on your own

   _____

4. (can) take the Tube / want to get around the city fast

   _____

5. (imperative) visit some museums / have enough time

   _____

6. (will) not be disappointed by the view / go up in the London Eye

   _____

b) *Which sentences are examples of advice, prediction or possibility? Write one word next to each sentence.*

LANGUAGE ⟨**16**⟩ **Your own ideas** (after Station 3)

Complete the sentences with your own ideas (use conditional clauses type 2)!

Example:
If I (know) everything: *If I knew everything, I would do very well in school!*

1. If I (win) lots of money: _____

2. If I (not have) homework for a week: _____

3. If I (not live) in Germany: _____

4. If I (wake up) earlier every day: _____

5. If I (be) 20 years old: _____

6. If I (see) a spaceship: _____

Green Line 2
Vorschläge zur Leistungsmessung
ISBN 978-3-12-834224-5

VIEWING **17** **A look at Cornwall**

a) *Watch the film. Which of these things do you learn about? Tick ✔ them. Be careful! Three topics aren't in the film.*

1. walking trails in Cornwall ☐

2. plant and animal life ☐

3. the weather in Cornwall ☐

4. the Celtic language in Cornwall ☐

5. Cornwall's location in England ☐

6. tourist attractions ☐

7. adventure holldays in Cornwall ☐

8. the geography of Cornwall ☐

9. tourists' reasons to visit Cornwall ☐

b) *Watch the film again. True or false? Tick ✔ the correct answer.*

	true	false
1. Cornwall is an island.	☐	☐
2. The sea is always not more than 20 miles away.	☐	☐
3. Tourists like Padstow because it's a nice fishing village.	☐	☐
4. There is no region in Britain that is warmer and sunnier than Cornwall.	☐	☐
5. People also call the north coast the 'Cornish Riviera'.	☐	☐
6. Land's End has its name because there's no more land that comes after it.	☐	☐
7. The Godrevy Lighthouse is on the west coast.	☐	☐
8. You won't see big waves along the north coast of Cornwall.	☐	☐
9. Not many people live on the north coast of Cornwall.	☐	☐
10. Cornwall isn't far from London.	☐	☐

▲ **c)** *Does the film make you want to visit Cornwall? Give three reasons why or why not.*

_____

_____

_____

 © Ernst Klett Verlag GmbH, Stuttgart 2015 | www.klett.de
Von dieser Druckvorlage ist die Vervielfältigung für den eigenen Unterrichtsgebrauch gestattet. Die Kopiergebühren sind abgegolten. Alle Rechte vorbehalten.

Green Line 2
Vorschläge zur Leistungsmessung
ISBN 978-3-12-834224-5

Unit 1 My friends and I

1 Listening: How were your holidays?

Either

a) 2. Home can be a dangerous place

b) 1. false (Emily went to an outdoor centre with her friends.) 2. true 3. false (They needed to go across a river to climb the gorge.) 4. true 5. true 6. false (The storm made the mountain climb more of an adventure.) 7. false (Emily broke her foot at home in the living room.)

Or

1. to an outdoor centre 2. She went gorge scrambling. 3. It was amazing and exciting. 4. She fell in. 5. There was a storm. 6. She broke her foot. 7. the living room/ home

2 Listening: Trouble on Red Nose Day

Either

a) A.–B. 4 C. 1 D. 2 E.–F. 3

b) 1. because he always chases everything
2. because he was sorry and embarrassed

Or

Samuel and Harry: c), d), f)

The older boys: b), e), h)

The girl: c), g), i)

The dog: a), c), i)

3 Reading: Our school trip

Either

a) 1. F 2. A 3. -- 4. E 5. D 6. B 7. C

b)

A Long but not boring	The class trip to Germany took a long time, but the students had fun on the coach.
B A home away from home	The host families met the students and took them home. Some things were different from England.
C Fun and great weather	The weather was great in Germany and the students did lots of outdoor activities.
D Adventure in the mountains	The students went climbing and swimming in the mountains.
E A trip to England	On the last day there was a football match Germany against England – Germany won. Germany wants to visit so England can try again.
F Not everything was better	The English students went back home after a great time in Germany. They were happy to be home!

Or

1. by coach 2. a little nervous 3. swam, had picnics, played ball games 4. what looked like a river 5. Germany 6. pools, weather, houses, food 7. They didn't like it (very much).

4 Reading: We were all winners

Either

a) + b) 1. false (Kate and Jenny raised money for charity, but they were in different groups.) 2. true 3. false (Emily is jealous of Kate because she always wins.) 4. false (The drinks weren't anything special.) 5. true 6. true 7. true

Or

	Kate	Emily
1. How did they make money?	sold hot drinks	sold cakes
2. Where did they make money?	on the market	at school
3. What did they do extra to win?	nothing	wore red noses / did funny things
4. How much money did they raise?	more than £54	£54
5. Who never wins, and why isn't it fair?	always wins	better singer, really tries but never wins

Klett

© Ernst Klett Verlag GmbH, Stuttgart 2015 | www.klett.de
Von dieser Druckvorlage ist die Vervielfältigung für den eigenen Unterrichtsgebrauch gestattet. Die Kopiergebühren sind abgegolten. Alle Rechte vorbehalten.

Green Line 2
Vorschläge zur Leistungsmessung
ISBN 978-3-12-834224-5

5 Writing: Red Nose Day

Lösungsvorschlag:
After the four friends made lots of money for Comic Relief they walked home. Sherlock was with them too. Then Jay wanted a drink, so they went into a café. They ate chips and drank tea because it was cold. They wanted to pay and go home but Jay found that he had no money. Oh no! It was very embarrassing! What did he do then? He went outside and sang on the street. He soon had some money and they all had a great time … again.

6 Writing: A travel report

Lösungsvorschlag "My last school trip":
For our last school trip we went to Berlin. We went there last year in November. We visited lots of famous sights like the "Reichstag" or the "Brandenburger Tor". We also went on a boat trip on the river Spree. We could see a lot of cool buildings from the boat! I really enjoyed the trip. It was very interesting and it was cool to learn some new things about the biggest German city.

Lösungsvorschlag "Sophie's school trip":
We went to the Black Mountains in Wales on our last school trip. That was two months ago. There were lots of interesting activities. We went mountain climbing and canoeing and we walked in the forest and saw lots of animals. The weather was nice below, but colder high up. I thought mountain climbing was exciting! I really enjoyed the trip!

7 Mediation: More than a holiday

Chris: I like to ride horses but I'm not very good at it. Is that a problem?
You: No, it says they also have courses for people.
Tina: What's that about teenagers and 13? We're 13 years old!
You: They have holidays for children, and teenagers 13 and older can go without their parents.
Chris: Where can you ride the horses?
You: You can ride them in the mountains.
Chris: You can ride alone in the mountains? That's dangerous!
You: No, the instructors go with you.

Chris: I see that you can also go kayaking. What else can you do there?
You: You can go mountain climbing too.
Tina: And what about in the evening?
You: They show films and you can dance in a disco.
Tina: What else is nice about the place?
You: It says it's one of the most beautiful places in Germany.
Chris: OK, it sounds good, but how do we get there?
You: Er, I don't know. There's no information about that.

8 Vocabulary: A report about Red Nose Day

report; yearbook; raised; best; sale; caught; proud of; pyjamas

9 Vocabulary: Look what happened!

1. famer 2. coach 3. driver 4. police 5. taxi 6. eye 7. nose 8. mechanic 9. postman

10 Vocabulary: A puzzle

1. real 2. confident 3. tall 4. nervous 5. anonymous 6. friendly 7. ↓high 7. →hard 8. shy 9. low 10. embarrassed

11 Language: Red Nose Day – A great idea!

made; sold; sang; wore; wanted; thought; came; saw; was; chatted; had; needed; helped; finished; started; did; raised; were

12 Language: Adventure holiday

1. Yes, she was. 2. No, he didn't. 3. No, he didn't. 4. Yes, they were. 5. Yes, it was. 6. No, he didn't. 7. No, he wasn't.

13 Language: What a joke!

Why were; How/When did you; Where did you; When/How long were; how much money did you; What did you

14 Language: Horses at an adventure centre

a) expensive; most expensive; smallest; young; younger; young
b) *Lösungsvorschlag:*
Paddy is the tallest of the three horses. He's also the oldest horse there. He's more expensive than Silver, but not as expensive as Megan. Silver is the cheapest of the three horses. He/She is taller than Megan, but not as tall as Paddy. Silver is the youngest horse there.

15 Language: Who was the bravest?

worse; nicer; most nervous; most awful; best; higher; scary; more confident; happier; bravest; braver

Green Line 2
Vorschläge zur Leistungsmessung
ISBN 978-3-12-834224-5

Unit 2 Let's discover TTS!

1 Listening: The Sign Language Club

Either
a) cat; sun; the alphabet; Hello!
b) 1. false 2. true 3. true 4. false 5. false

Or
1. last year 2. the alphabet 3. the months 4. She wanted to talk to her brother (who can't hear).
5. They make a lot of mistakes. 6. on Wednesdays after school

2 Listening: Using a timetable

Either

Monday	Subject	Room	Why?
8.50	Technology	1. **T24**	2. **the sound is great**
9.50	3. **Technology**	T17	
10.50	**Break**		
11.10	4. **Maths**	G40	5. **more computers**
12.10	6. **English**	B12	7. **the Drama class needs more tables**
13.10	**Lunch**		
14.00	Dance	Studio B	8. **a window is broken (in Studio A)**

Or
1. c 2. c 3. b 4. a 5. a, c 6. a, c

3 Reading: A History project

Either
1. Samuel Pepys 2. Sir Francis Drake 3. Thomas Tallis
4. Samuel Pepys 5. Thomas Tallis 6. Francis Drake

Or
1. He can't find enough information about Thomas Tallis.
2. church music 3. He sailed around the world. 4. food and jewellery 5. friends and neighbours, life in London, historical events

4 Reading: Which club?

Either
1. B 2. C 3. A 4. C 5. A 6. B

Or
a, b) 1. true 2. false (It's hard.) 3. false (You learn a new dance each week.) 4. true 5. false (You need to bring a box or a bag.) 6. false (They make food from different parts of the world/ different countries.)

5 Writing: Partner school

Lösungsvorschlag:
Dear Mrs Brown,
My aunt told me that you are looking for a German partner school for your exchange programme. This is why I'm writing to you to tell you about our school. We have classes like Maths, PE (we call this Sport), Music, German and Art. We also have language classes like French and English. I like my English class the best because the language is fun to learn. Art class is good too, because I like to paint pictures. There are lots of clubs at my school, like the Music Club, the Art Club and the Book Club. I'm in the Music Club, and we sing and dance and have lots of fun. There's also the Basketball Club and the Football Club. I play basketball at the Basketball Club. But we play lots of other games in Sport too. It's a great school, and we hope you can come and find this out too!
Can you please tell us more about TTS, please? What classes and clubs has your school got? We'd like to hear from you!
Thank you very much!
Jule

Green Line 2
Vorschläge zur Leistungsmessung
ISBN 978-3-12-834224-5

6 Writing: School trips and stories

Lösungsvorschlag:

a) Hi Holly,

I hope we can go to the theatre for our class trip! Then we can see actors acting what we're reading in English class! I like to watch TV and to go to the cinema, but I like the theatre the best! It's more real and exciting when an actor is in front of me. It's much more exciting than looking at pieces of art! And I don't like swimming! We have to do that in Sport, so I don't want to go on a trip to do it even more! Where do you want to go?

b) *Individuelle S-Antwort*

7 Mediation: School clubs

Lösungsvorschlag:

Hi students in 6B! You've got some great clubs at your school! We do too! There are 15 clubs at our school. Some meet in the lunch break. There's the Book Club, where one person makes a suggestion for a new book every week. Everyone reads the book and then they discuss it the next week. The most popular club is the School Magazine Club. It meets on Thursdays at 1 o'clock. First the members decide which articles and pictures they want to use. Then they do interviews, write articles and take funny pictures. Everyone loves our school magazine!

8 Mediation: A school trip!

Hollys Besuch im Kunstmuseum mit ihrer Klasse war sehr aufregend! Einige ihrer Mitschüler mochten die moderne Kunst nicht, aber Holly fand sie toll. Sie hat sich gerade ein Bild angeschaut, als Jay sie angerempelt hat. Sie ist dann gestolpert und über die Linie vor dem Gemälde getreten und der Alarm ging los! Der Museumswärter und ihr Lehrer kamen angerannt und waren total aufgeregt. Jay und Holly haben ihnen erklärt, dass es ein Versehen war und es ihnen leid tut. Sie haben ihnen gesagt, dass sie vorsichtiger sein sollen.

9 Vocabulary: What we do in lessons

1. g 2. f 3. a 4. b 5. h 6. c 7. d

10 Vocabulary: Club flyers

1. steal 2. interested; Birdwatching 3. welcome 4. paintings 5. Architect 6. forward 7. dancers; started
8. wildlife; Eco

11 Language: The Science Museum

which/that; who/that; which/that; which/that; which/that; whose; whose

12 Language: We won!

1. The players who we were playing against were from West London.
2. The other team had a captain whose name was Will.
3. They wore football shoes which/that were red and white.
4. The football shoes which/that our team wore were yellow and blue.
5. There were students from our school whose cheering helped us play better! / The students whose cheering helped us play better were from our school.
6. We have a great captain who always knows what to do.

13 Language: The show

a) 1. which/that 2. who/that 3. which/that 4. which/that 5. who/that 6. who/that
b) 1; 4

14 Language: What were they doing?

1. Luke was playing football with another boy.
2. Olivia was writing a text / playing with her phone.
3. Jay was dancing (and singing).
4. Dave was looking at/reading a (computer) magazine.
5. Gwen was talking to Holly.
6. A bird was building a nest.
7. The sun was shining.

15 Language: A technology lesson

was walking; was showing; was he showing; were asking; were designing; weren't working; were you doing; wasn't doing; was thinking

16 Language: Scary ghosts!

didn't want; was talking; were going; made; wasn't; was laughing; was talking; was watching; saw; jumped

Green Line 2
Vorschläge zur Leistungsmessung
ISBN 978-3-12-834224-5

Unit 3 London is amazing!

1 Listening: Holiday plans

Either

1. it's always so boring 2. tourist attractions 3. watch a football game 4. see/buy new computer games/go in costume as your favourite character/see famous people/meet people that make the games, comics 5. £20 6. can go to the Comic Con

Or

a) + b) 1. false (Dave's aunt and uncle are going to visit him.) 2. false (They want to visit all the tourist attractions in London.) 3. true 4. false (Dave thinks football is boring.) 5. true 6. true 7. false (At the beginning, Dave thought he wasn't going to do anything good.)

2 Listening: A tour of London

Either

1. c 2. a, b 3. c 4. a 5. b 6. a, c

Or

a) 1: Buckingham Palace 2: Hyde Park 3: Royal Albert Hall 4: Science Museum 5: Westminster Cathedral

b) 1. 775 2. a swimming pool 3. about £17 4. almost 500 years old 5. the boating lake, concerts 6. 1871

3 Reading: A trip to Hampton Court Palace

Either

1. e 2. d 3. h 4. g 5. f 6. a 7. c 8. b

Or

a) 1. Holly, Olivia 2. Desmond 3. Catherine Howard 4. King Henry the Eighth 5. Lucy 6. Holly 7. the actor

b) *Lösungsvorschlag:*

The ending is surprising because Holly thinks it was the actor who screamed. But she says it wasn't her and she didn't hear the scream. Was it really the ghost of Catherine Howard?

4 Reading: Lots of fun in London with just a little money

Either

a) + b) 1. false (You can do a lot of interesting things in London even if you don't have a lot of money.) 2. true 3. false (You can find three museums at South Kensington.) 4. false (You can see lots of interesting plants and animals there.) 5. false (The Victoria and Albert Museum is an art gallery, but you can see other things there too.) 6. true

Or

1. castles and wax museums 2. on school trips 3. they're near each other and free
4.–5. The Victoria and Albert Museum 6. The Science Museum

5 Writing: A special place

Lösungsvorschlag „My tourist sight":
I really like the park in my town. It's very big and you can go cycling, play football or just meet your friends there. There's a lake too and you can take boat rides. In summer, there are always lots of tourists. The café near the lake is very popular. My friends and I like to buy ice cream there!

Lösungsvorschlag „The London Eye":
The London Eye is an important tourist attraction in London. It's on the south side of the Thames, opposite the Houses of Parliament. It's a big ferris wheel – one of the biggest ferris wheels in the world! It's 135 metres high and from the top you can see London from above. The journey takes 30 minutes and the wheel doesn't usually stop. A ticket costs £29.95, but you can buy them online for £26.96.

6 Writing: Be careful!

Lösungsvorschlag Bild 1:

Woman: Oh, excuse me … Be careful!
Man: Oops! Thank you, that was really close!
Woman: Are you OK?
Man: Yes, I am. Sorry, I didn't see your bag.
Woman: Yes, that's a really big wax figure! What are you doing with it?
Man: I need to take it to the museum. I'm already late. Sorry again. Bye!
Woman: No problem. Bye!

Lösungsvorschlag Bild 2:

Mother: Zoe, please stop talking on the phone and come back here.
Zoe: Oh, mum … it's so boring here!
Mother: Hey, that isn't very polite! This man is talking about really interesting things.
Beefeater: Thank you. That's true. The history of this place is very … Oh, be careful, young lady! There's a raven behind you.
Zoe: What? Where … ouch! OK, I'm going to listen now …

Green Line 2
Vorschläge zur Leistungsmessung
ISBN 978-3-12-834224-5

7 Mediation: Queen Elizabeth Olympic Park

Opa: Der Park sieht riesig aus und ich bin nicht so gut zu Fuß. Muss ich überall hinlaufen?
Du: Nein, man kann auch eine Bootstour machen und so alles sehen.
Oma: Und wie kommt man überhaupt hin?
Du: Man kann mit dem Zug oder Bus oder mit dem Auto hinfahren.
Oma: Stratford – liegt im Osten von London, oder? Was ist das für ein Stadtteil?
Du: Ein Stadtteil, in dem es früher Probleme gab. Jetzt hat er sich aber zum Guten geändert und ist eine beliebte Londoner Sehenswürdigkeit.
Opa: Was kann man dort machen?
Du: Man kann schwimmen gehen oder die anderen Sportstadien benutzen.
Opa: Und gibt es im Oktober, wenn wir da sind, irgendwelche Veranstaltungen dort?
Du: Ja, es gibt ein Rollstuhltennisturnier und ein Basketballspiel.
Oma: Und falls es regnet, können wir irgendwo hingehen ohne Sport treiben zu müssen?
Du: Ja, es gibt dort viele Cafés!

8 Vocabulary: Adventure on the Tube . . .

public transport; adventure; get around; wheelchair; stop; upset; offered; change onto; top up

9 Vocabulary: Opposites

1. south 2. con 3. far 4. everybody 5. large/huge 6. to push

10 Vocabulary: The problems of a Beefeater

Beefeater; prison; raven master; ravens; bite; careful; safe

11 Language: Ready for Mum's birthday party?

isn't going to clean; are going to clean; is going to go shopping; aren't going to go; are going to make; isn't going to make; are going to wrap; are going to decorate; is going to cook; going to have

12 Language: Sally asks about Will's weekend plans

1. What are you going to do at the weekend? 2. We're going to go to London. 3. Are you going to visit Buckingham Palace? 4. No, we aren't going to visit any tourist attractions 5. Why aren't you going to do that? 6. We're going to watch a football match.

13 Language: Trafalgar Square

1. A woman is going to take a photo of a man. 2. The man is going to fall into the water. 3. Two children are going to buy an ice cream. 4. Two women are going to give a musician some money. 5. A musician is going to get some money.

14 Language: Let's eat something!

nothing; anybody/anyone; any/some; somewhere; anybody/anyone; anywhere; somebody/someone; any; some; Everybody/Everyone; nowhere; somewhere; everybody/everyone; something/anything

15 Language: Holly at the Tower

famous; excitedly; bored; quietly; nervous; happy; sadly; careful; quickly; hard; hungrily; interesting; fast; slowly; nervous; impressed

16 Language: The boys

1. faster 2. most quickly 3. better 4. more easily 5. the hardest 6. harder

17 Viewing: A look at the Thames

a) 1: The Houses of Parliament 2: Big Ben 3: The London Eye 4: The Shard 5: The Tower Bridge 6: O₂Arena 7: Thames Barrier
b) 1. false 2. false 3. true 4. true 5. false 6. true
c) 1. a 2. c 3. b 4. c

Green Line 2
Vorschläge zur Leistungsmessung
ISBN 978-3-12-834224-5

Unit 4 Sport is good for you

1 Listening: What's important?

Either

a) + b) 1. false (Jack called David from (the) hospital.)
2. false (Jack hasn't broken anything.) 3. false (He fell off his skateboard in the park.) 4. true 5. true 6. true 7. false (Harry thinks the most important thing is that Jack is OK.)

Or

1. because he's had an accident. 2. He fell over. / He hurt his leg when he was skating. 3. He can't play football 4. Jack is their best player. 5. all of them 6. very well 7. that Jack is OK

2 Listening: A dramatic sea rescue

Either

a) 1. The boat was small. 2. There were four people in the boat. 3. Nobody was hurt. 4. The reporter and Louise talk at 4 p.m. 5. The eyewitness is a woman. 6. She has got a dog.

b) 1. The tide pushed them out to sea. 2. She called the emergency service. 3. The lifeboat got to them quickly/ saved them.

Or

1. Louise Hudson is ~~a radio reporter~~. → an eyewitness
2. She talks to a reporter ~~on Saturday at 5 p.m.~~ → on Sunday at 4 p.m.
3. She was ~~phoning a friend~~ when she saw that the boat was in trouble. → walking her dog
4. The tide was pushing the boat ~~to shore.~~ → out to sea
5. Louise called ~~the lifeboat station.~~ → the emergency services
6. The family was cold and scared but not hurt. → correct

3 Reading: Running can be dangerous

Either

1. d 2. g 3. a 4. e 5. f 6. c 7. b

Or

1. He wants to go for a run in the park. 2. He goes with him because running in the dark can be dangerous. 3. Luke and his dad are chatting and laughing and the young man is listening to music. 4. Mr Elliot thinks he has stolen his phone. 5. Mr Elliot has stolen the man's phone.

4 Reading: The big match!

Either

1. that he isn't on the team 2. upset 3. he isn't playing well enough 4. both teams are nervous 5. 0:0 6. Jack has hurt his leg 7. kicks the ball into the goal/net and wins the game for TTS

Or

1. false 2. false 3. true 4. true 5. false 6. false 7. true

5 Writing: Sports at schools in Germany

Lösungsvorschlag:

Dear Daniel,

Thank you for your e-mail and the funny photos you sent me of your Sports Day. They were great! You asked me about PE in Germany. Well, at my school we have four PE lessons each week. I have PE on Mondays and Wednesdays. We often learn to play ball games like basketball or volleyball. The boys in my class like basketball, but most of the girls like volleyball better. My favourite sport is dancing. I often go to hip hop dance class after school. It's really cool!

Write back soon!

Leyla

6 Writing: Be careful when you run!

Lösungsvorschlag:

a)

Doctor: Good morning, young man. How can I help you?
Boy: I've had an accident and I've hurt my leg.
Doctor: How did it happen?
Boy: I was running in the mini marathon when two people in animal costumes got in my way and I fell.

Doctor: Can you walk on your leg?
Boy: Yes, but it hurts.
Doctor: Let me have a look at it … Oh, yes, you've twisted your ankle but it isn't broken. Here's a prescription for an ointment. Be careful for the next few days.

Green Line 2
Vorschläge zur Leistungsmessung
ISBN 978-3-12-834224-5

b)

Luke:	What? No, that can't be. Oh no, that means … Dad, you've stolen that man's phone!
Mrs Elliot:	You've *what*?
Mr Elliot:	Oh, no! I'm so sorry now. I really thought I had my phone with me when we were running, so I thought that young man stole it when we ran into each other. It looked like it …
Luke:	What do we do now? You have to give the phone back!
Mrs Elliot:	We should go to the police. Maybe the man went to talk to the police too and they know who he is now and where we can find him.
Mr Elliot:	Yes, that's a good idea. I really want to give the phone back and say sorry. Let's go!
Luke:	OK, Dad.
Mrs Elliot:	I'm coming with you this time! I can't let you two go out alone again!

7 Mediation: Children and health

The text says that a hundred years ago children got more exercise. And they were fitter. In the mornings they walked to school because there were no cars. In the afternoons they played outside. Or they worked in the fields. Today many teenagers spend their free time in front of the TV, on the internet or with video games.

8 Mediation: At the doctor's

Dad:	Sage ihm, dass ich gestern einen Fahrradunfall hatte und dass ich mein Bein verletzt habe.
You:	Yesterday my father had a bike accident and he hurt his leg.
Doctor:	Oh I'm sorry! Why didn't you come right away? Have you taken any pills for the pain yet?
You:	Er will wissen, warum bist du nicht gleich zu ihm gekommen bist. Hast du schon Schmerztabletten genommen?
Dad:	Noch nicht. Könnte er mir bitte ein Rezept für Tabletten und eine Salbe geben?
You:	Not yet. Could you give him a prescription for some pills and some ointment, please?
Doctor:	Of course, but first I'd like to take a careful look at your leg.
You:	Natürlich, aber zuerst möchte er sich dein Bein sorgfältig anschauen.

9 Vocabulary: Sport verbs

1. to run 2. to kick 3. to hit 4. to throw/to pass 5. to catch 6. to lose

10 Vocabulary: Parts of the body

1. head 2. eye 3. mouth 4. shoulder 5. arm 6. stomach 7. finger 8. leg 9. ankle 10. feet

11 Vocabulary: Saying it differently

1. sick 2. a headache 3. pain 4. have a look at 5. caught 6. twisted

12 Vocabulary: Where's Luke?

caught; fever; cough; headache; arms; pain; legs; doctor yet; have a look; prescription

13 Vocabulary: Molly's story

leg; accident; running; races; experience; what it's like; almost; hurts; yet; award; cheered

14 Language: Running with the friends

1. Have Luke and Jay ever heard of the mini marathon? – No, they haven't.
2. Has Dave ever run in a marathon? – No, he hasn't.
3. Have Luke and his friends ever trained in Greenwich Park? – Yes, they have.
4. Has Olivia ever hurt her ankle before a race? – Yes, she has.
5. Has Gwen ever lost a race? – Yes, she has.
6. Has she ever won a marathon? – No, she hasn't.

15 Language: An interview with Jim Comber

Have you ever played; have; have/'ve never played; Have you met; have; have/'ve already done; Have the Tigers ever bought; have; have/'ve never paid; Has the trainer given; has already organised; Have you started; haven't

16 Language: Daniel Best

has already won; started; was; entered; didn't win; made; won; didn't do; hasn't become; has already earned

17 Language: Before school

Have you finished; have; 've already put; 've just found; was; Did you take; didn't; forgot; didn't need; wasn't; didn't have; did; did; was; haven't forgotten

Green Line 2
Vorschläge zur Leistungsmessung
ISBN 978-3-12-834224-5

Unit 5 Stay in touch

1 Listening: Talking about advice

Either

1. Filip 2. John 3. Steve 4. John 5. Filip 6. Filip 7. Steve

Or

a) + b) 1. false (John posted party photos of his friends.) 2. true 3. false (Ruby thinks John's friends aren't overreacting.) 4. false (Filip wants to stay out later at weekends.) 5. false (Holly and Olivia both can't stay out later than Filip.) 6. true 7. true 8. false (Ruby thinks a smartphone is a good idea for a birthday present.)

2 Listening: A school project

Either

a) + b) 4; – (Henry didn't want to throw his smartphone away./Henry says he wants to keep his smartphone.); 1; – (Henry didn't use his smartphone in secret.); 3; 2

Or

1. kept his smartphone for the week 2. were having fun without him 3. his mother and brother 4. face-to-face 5. had a lot to talk about 6. most people stay in touch 7. not so much

3 Reading: Stay safe online!

Either

1. D 2. C 3. E 4. – 5. A 6. F 7. B

Or

a) + b) + c) 1. true (ll. 8–9) 2. false (l. 12: Don't be rude in your e-mails.) 3. true (ll. 3–5) 4. false (l. 2: Don't tell anyone the sports team or clubs you belong to.) 5. false (ll. 10–11: If you don't know your online friends, they aren't your real friends.) 6. true (ll. 6–7)

4 Reading: Keeping in touch

Either

1. b 2. b 3. a, c 4. a, b, 5. b 6. a, c

Or

1. lonely; embarrassed; stared; whispered 2. things went better 3. everyone asked her questions; 4. you all enjoy the same activity and you have a lot to talk about.

5 Writing: I want a party!

a) *Lösungsvorschlag:*

Hi Ben,

The school trip was great. There were lots of cool things to see and do at the museum. I'm sorry you're feeling so upset about your birthday. I understand that the situation is hard for you. Have you tried talking to your parents about your feelings? My advice is to find a compromise. Why don't you enjoy your birthday during your weekend by the sea with your family and celebrate with your friends on the next weekend? I hope I could help you. Write back soon.

6 Writing: Agony aunt contest

Individuelle S-Antwort

7 Mediation: Advice about different interests

Kevin: Hi Tom! Uh, what's the matter! You look really sad!

You: Kevin möchte wissen was los ist, weil du sehr traurig aussiehst.

Tom: Meine Freunde wollen in ihrer Freizeit nur Sport machen! Ich bin nicht gut in Sport und es macht mir nicht viel Spaß. Ich weiß nicht, was ich tun soll!

You: His friends only want to do sport in their free time. He's not good at sport and he doesn't really enjoy it. He doesn't know what to do.

Kevin: Have you tried talking to them about it? Maybe you can find a compromise! Why don't you try to have fun together in other ways? You could go to a film or play video games …

You: Er möchte wissen, ob du versucht hast mit deinen Freunden darüber zu reden. Vielleicht könntet ihr einen Kompromiss finden. Warum versucht ihr nicht auf andere Weise Spaß miteinander zu haben? Ihr könntet ins Kino gehen oder Videospiele spielen …

Tom: Ich kann sie nicht dazu bringen etwas zu machen, was sie nicht machen wollen!

You: He says he can't make them do what they don't want to do.

Kevin: But you can't know what they're going to say when you haven't asked them yet! The next step is to call them, or if you're too nervous, why don't you text them?

Green Line 2
Vorschläge zur Leistungsmessung
ISBN 978-3-12-834224-5

You: Er sagt, dass du nicht wissen kannst, was sie sagen, wenn du sie noch nicht gefragt hast. Der nächste Schritt ist sie anzurufen. Oder, wenn du zu nervös bist, könntest du ihnen eine SMS schreiben.

Tom: Ich hoffe, dass sie nicht denken, dass ich blöd bin, aber ich werde es trotzdem versuchen.

You: He hopes that his friends don't think that he's stupid, but he's going to try anyway.

8 Vocabulary: Media collocations

1. f 2. a, c 3. g 4. a, c 5. b, d 6. b, d 7. g 8. e, h

9 Vocabulary: What should you do?

1. b, c 2. c 3. a, b 4. a, c 5. a 6. c 7. a 8. b, c

10 Language: Ideas that changed the world!

after; because; As soon as/When; like; until/before; like; before

11 Language: Project time

don't you; can't we; haven't you; do we; have you; aren't I; didn't we; has he

12 Language: Gwen's life at home

'm able to; 'm not able to; 're able to; aren't allowed to; 're allowed to; 'm not able to; don't have to; 'm allowed to

13 Language: When my dad was young ...

weren't able to; had to; was allowed to; wasn't able to; was able to; wasn't able to; didn't have to; had to; wasn't allowed to

14 Language: Giving advice

1. You should write them in your planner. 2. You could read history books or go to a history museum. 3. You could take part in the Music or Dance Club. 4. You shouldn't pass on secrets. 5. You should go to the doctor. 6. You shouldn't be too self-critical.

15 Language: Looking for advice

should; can; can't; should/need to/must/have to; needn't; had to; wasn't able/allowed to; shouldn't; was allowed to; didn't have to; can/should

Unit 6 Goodbye Greenwich

1 Listening: A family trip

Either
Cornwall: F, H Ireland: D, G Edinburgh: A, E Cardiff: B, C

Or
1. a 2. b, c 3. b 4. c 5. a, b 6. b

2 Listening: The Newcastle Morning Show

Either
1. it'll be warm and sunny 2. Sunday 3. there'll be storms, rain and wind 4. tunnels 5. the afternoon 6. there'll be lots of clouds 7. next week

Or
a) Saturday: b, g, i, j Sunday: a, c, d, e, h, k
b) + c) 1. true 2. false (There will be storms and rain and wind on Sunday morning.) 3. true 4. false (You can learn about Newcastle's history in the Victoria Tunnel.) 5. false (It will be colder on Sunday than on Saturday.) 6. true

3 Reading: Moving house for a year

Either

Person	How does he/she feel?	Examples from the text
mum	nervous/excited	"Mum is already panicking" / "She's always happy if she can organise something"
sister	excited/happy	"my sister is writing lists too, ... for all the clothes she'll get in New York"
dad	excited/happy	"my dad is always running around and singing New York songs"
Terry	sad/a little excited	"I'll miss our class trip, our parties, our crazy weekends – and you all" / "maybe it'll be an adventure" / "I guess it will be exciting"

Green Line 2
Vorschläge zur Leistungsmessung
ISBN 978-3-12-834224-5

Or

1. c 2. c 3. b, c 4. c 5. a, c 6. b

4 Reading: Travel, but carefully!

Either

Good things about travel: a, d, g, n
Bad things about travel: e, h, i, m
Possible solutions: b, c, f, k, j, l

Or

a) 3., 4., 5.

b) 1. The text says you should think about how you travel so it isn't (so) bad for the environment. 2. The text doesn't say that you shouldn't travel at all. It says that you should travel in a careful way. 6. This person doesn't care about recycling when he/she is travelling. The text says that you should put your rubbish in the right place / throw it away in the right way.

5 Writing: Holidays in England or Wales

Lösungsvorschlag:

Dear Tom,

Hi from Cornwall! It's great here. Yesterday we visited a small fishing village. We saw lots of boats and ate fish. We also went to the beach and went swimming in the sea. Tomorrow we're going to visit Cardiff. The weather has been really warm and sunny all the time – much sunnier than in Germany! The people here are very nice. Some of them even speak Welsh! I'll be back home next week.

Talk to you soon, Lotta

6 Writing: What will/won't my life be like in 2030?

Lösungsvorschlag:

1. I will/won't work with computers / I'll have a good job.
2. I will/won't have a family / children.
3. I will/won't travel a lot / the world.
4. I will/won't have / I'll live in a house / I'll live in a flat.
5. I'll still be friends with my best friend.
6. I'll have a cool, fast car.

7 Mediation: Travelling by train

Tourist: Wir müssen ganz schnell nach Liverpool. Wann fährt der nächste Zug?
Du: Der nächste Zug fährt um 3 Uhr 10.
Tourist: Oje! Wir müssen auch noch Fahrkarten kaufen. Welche späteren Verbindungen gibt es denn?
Du: Die nächste Verbindung ist um 3 Uhr 40.
Tourist: Müssen wir umsteigen? Wenn ja, wann fährt der Zug weiter?
Du: Man muss in Crewe umsteigen. Der Zug fährt um 5 Uhr 32 von dort weiter.
Tourist: In Ordnung. Und wie lange brauchen wir dann noch bis Liverpool?
Du: 39 Minuten.
Tourist: Wie viel kosten die Tickets für zwei Erwachsene für die Hin- und Rückfahrt?
Du: 618 Pfund.
Tourist: Und was kostet das für beide Kinder?
Du: 309 Pfund.
Tourist: Vielen Dank!

8 Mediation: Another trip by train

Man: Good afternoon. How may I help you?
Papa: Frag ihn bitte wann der nächste Zug nach Liverpool abfährt.
Du: When does the next train to Liverpool depart, please?
Man: That's at 3:10 p.m. The train gets to Liverpool at 5:45 p.m.
Du: Um 10 nach 3. Dieser Zug kommt um Viertel vor 6 in Liverpool an.
Papa: Aber wir müssen etwas essen bevor wir einsteigen. Welche späteren Verbindungen gibt es denn? Aber ich möchte, dass wir vor 7 Uhr abends in Liverpool ankommen!
Du: We'd like to eat something before we get on the train. Is there a later train that gets to Liverpool before 7 p.m./seven in the evening?
Man: There are also trains leaving at 3:40 p.m. and at 4:10 p.m. The train at 4:10 gets to Liverpool at 6:44 p.m.
Du: Es gibt auch noch Züge um 20 vor 4 und 10 nach 4. Der spätere Zug kommt um 6 Uhr 44 in Liverpool an.
Mum: Muss man umsteigen bei der Verbindung um 4:10?

Green Line 2
Vorschläge zur Leistungsmessung
ISBN 978-3-12-834224-5

Du:	Do we have to change if we take the train at 4:10?
Man:	Yes, you'll need to once.
Du:	Ja, wir müssen einmal umsteigen.
Mum:	Und wie viel kosten die Tickets für die Hin- und Rückfahrt?
Du:	How much is a return ticket?
Man:	They cost £309 for adults and £154.50 for children older than five.
Du:	309 Pfund für Erwachsene und 154 Pfund 50 für Kinder ab 5 Jahren.
Papa:	Sind die Tickets immer so teuer?
Du:	Are the tickets always so expensive?
Man:	The tickets are cheaper if you book them early, or if you can travel on different days and at different times.
Du:	Sie sind billiger, wenn man früher bucht oder an einem anderen Tag oder zu einer anderen Zeit reist.
Du	(bedankst dich für seine Hilfe): Thank you very much for your help.

9 Vocabulary: Places and what you can do there

Lösungsvorschlag:
1. city/town: visit a museum; go shopping; go to a festival
2. seaside: go for a walk; go swimming; go windsurfing
3. mountains: go climbing; go mountain biking; go pony trekking

10 Vocabulary: Weather words

1. rain 2. cold 3. lightning 4. clouds 5. sun 6. warm

11 Vocabulary: A weekend trip

book; travel agent's; depends on; change; depart; arrive; return; fare; per

12 Vocabulary: Guess the word!

1. announcement 2. Wild 3. get to know 4. customers 5. monuments 6. coastline 7. from around the world 8. accent 9. Irish 10. cross

13 Language: The friends' weekend trip to Cornwall

'll have; won't rain; will – bring; 'll be; 'll take; 'll go; Will – come; 'll buy; won't be able

14 Language: What they do in different situations

1. they can/will watch TV/a film 2. they can/will go swimming 3. He can/will win the race 4. you should go to bed / sleep 5. you should call the emergency service 6. You should eat the chips

15 Language: A trip to London

a) + b):
1. If you go to London, you'll have a good time. / You'll have a good time if you go to London. (prediction)
2. If you want to go in the summer, you should book your trip early. / You should book your trip early if you want to go in the summer. (advice)
3. If you aren't into tours, you can go everywhere on your own. / You can go everywhere on your own if you aren't into tours. (possibility)
4. If you want to get around the city fast, you can take the Tube. / You can take the Tube if you want to get around the city fast. (possibility)
5. If you have enough time, visit some museums. / Visit some museums if you have enough time. (advice)
6. If you go up in the London Eye, you won't be disappointed by the view. / You won't be disappointed by the view if you go up in the London Eye. (prediction)

<16> Language: Your own ideas

Lösungsvorschlag:
1. If I won lots of money, I would/I'd have a huge party with all of my friends.
2. If I didn't have homework for a week, I would/I'd be really happy.
3. If I didn't live in Germany, I would/I'd live in Scotland.
4. If I woke up earlier every day, I could have breakfast at home before school.
5. If I was 20 years old, I could go to school by car.
6. If I saw a spaceship, I would/I'd call a reporter!

17 Viewing: A look at Cornwall

a) 3, 5, 6, 8, 9
b) 1. false 2. true 3. true 4. true 5. false 6. true 7. false 8. false 9. true 10. false
c) *Individuelle S-Antworten*

Green Line 2
Vorschläge zur Leistungsmessung
ISBN 978-3-12-834224-5

Unit 1

Warm up: • Which outdoor sports/activities did you do last July or August (in your school holidays)?
• Are there some sports/activities that you like more than others? Why?

Monologues: Model answers

1. A boy and girl are by a lake, and they are riding their bikes. It looks fun to ride here! There are mountains by the lake, and you can see a boat too. The girl is wearing a blue T-shirt and the boy is wearing an orange T-shirt. They look happy. I'd like/wouldn't like to go there because …
Individuelle S-Antworten

2. These children are gorge scrambling! A girl and a boy are helping another boy into the water. Three children have only their feet in the water. The three children below them are standing where the water is higher. All of the children are wearing warm clothes because the water is cold. They're having a great adventure! I'd like/wouldn't like to go there because …
Individuelle S-Antworten

3. The children are visiting a farm. You can see the farmer's house and also where the animals live. One child is helping the farmer. One girl is next to a sheep. Another girl is with the chickens. Three girls are riding horses. A man is helping one girl. I'd like/wouldn't like to go there because …
Individuelle S-Antworten

4. These children are walking in the mountains. A girl and a boy are looking at a map. The girl is saying something to the boy. Another boy is pointing to a small village below, and three others are looking to where he is pointing. There's a church in the middle of the village and a few houses around it. The children have lots of things with them. I'd like/wouldn't like to go there because …
Individuelle S-Antworten

Dialogues: Useful questions and phrases

• I think our classmates would like …
• What about a …?
• A trip to … is a great idea!
• Let's …
• My suggestion is that we …
• What's your idea / What do you think?
• Do you like my idea?

• That's a fun/good idea!
• That's a good place, but …
• Some people like/don't like …
• Do you have a better idea?
• Maybe we also need to think about …
• Is this place good for all of our classmates?
• That's cheap/expensive.

Dialogues: Model answers

A I really like the idea of a class trip to Explore Outdoor Centre! You can go bike riding and swimming and boating there, or play football – there's fun and adventure for everyone! And I don't think £250 for a week is expensive. And I don't like cooking, so it's good that we don't have to make our meals. What do you think?

B What about a class trip to the Wales Activity Camp? Many of our classmates like different things, but everyone can find something here. There's mountain walking, tennis and football for the people who like sports, but also town and museum visits for the people who are into culture. Do you like my idea?

▲ **Role play:** Imagine you and your partner are one of the people in one of these pictures. What's happening? What are you saying to each other?

Green Line 2
Vorschläge zur Leistungsmessung
ISBN 978-3-12-834224-5

Unit 2

Warm up: • Which clubs are there at your school?
             • Which club(s) are you a member of?
             • Do you think it's important for schools to have clubs? Why or why not?

Monologues: Model answers

1. This is the Art Club. People were talking about their art/mangas/drawings. Two students were talking to the teacher. Other students were looking at pictures on the walls. One student was drawing a picture. Another student was painting. They were enjoying/interested in what they were doing.	**2.** This is the Music Club. Lots of students were singing together. One student was even singing alone in front of the group. Another student was playing the saxophone, and the teacher was playing guitar with the group too (*die Gitarre*). Most of the students were clapping their hands. They were having a great time!
3. This is the Basketball Club. There were two girls on the team with the yellow T-shirts. The other team had orange T-shirts. One boy from the orange team was throwing the ball into the basket. The members of his team were cheering. One boy from the yellow team wasn't playing. Other members of the yellow team didn't look happy.	**4.** This is the Cinema/Film Club. Students were watching a film. A few students were whispering to each other. Some were laughing a little. One student was drinking from his drink, and other students were eating popcorn or crisps. Most students were interested in the film / Maybe the students who were whispering were bored.

Dialogues: Useful questions and phrases

• Let's join the … Club! • I like the … Club. What about you? • Do you know something about the … Club? • Which club are you interested in? • Which club do you want to choose? • Sorry, but I don't want to join the … Club because … • I like the … Club more because I'm good at…	• I have a problem with that idea because I'm: a bad singer/not good at sports/not good at drawing, painting/not interested in art/not very creative/not into films … • Maybe we can find out more about the clubs before we decide. • That's a great idea! / That's the club for us! • Great! I can't wait till the club meets!

Dialogues: Model answers

1. Let's join the Art Club! You like drawing, and I like painting, so there's something for you and me. And we can get new ideas from other people who like the same things! What do you think? *Individuelle S-Antworten*	**2.** I don't think I want to join the Music Club. I like to sing, but only when I'm alone. I'm shy so I don't want to be in a show in front of other students! And I can't play another instrument (*Instrument*).What about another club? *Individuelle S-Antworten*
3. What about the Basketball Club! It's a really fun game, and we're good at it when we play in PE! The team won every game last year! The other members and the teacher are very nice. Do you want to join this club too? *Individuelle S-Antworten*	**4.** Sorry, but I don't want to join the Film Club. I don't want to watch boring films that other club members choose! I can watch the films I like at home or in the cinema. Let's find out more about the other clubs. *Individuelle S-Antworten*

 Discussion: One of you is the teacher and the other is a student. Choose one of the four clubs. The teacher wants to stop this club at the end of the school year, and he/she tells you why. You aren't happy about this! Discuss this with him/her and decide what you can/want to do about it.

Green Line 2
Vorschläge zur Leistungsmessung
ISBN 978-3-12-834224-5

Unit 3

Warm up: • What do you know about London (places, people, events …)? How do you know this?
(visit to London/books/TV …)
• Would you like to visit London? Why or why not?

Monologues: Model answers

1. This is the British Museum. Here you can see lots of interesting and amazing things from many different countries in the world. And the museum is free! This is a very big museum, so it's good to plan a lot of time for your visit! I'd like to go to … because … *Individuelle S-Antworten*	**1.** This is Buckingham Palace. Here you can see where the Queen lives (sometimes). This is only one of her houses. You can also see the Changing of the Guards. Maybe you can even see a member of the royal family! I'd like to go to … because … *Individuelle S-Antworten*
2. This is Covent Garden. There's always a lot to see and do here! You can see great street shows with music, comedy, or people who do amazing tricks like juggling on bikes. There are also shops and cafés, and lots of people to watch! I'd like to go to … because … *Individuelle S-Antworten*	**2.** This is Hyde Park. Here you can relax under one of the big trees, sit by the lake or you can walk around. There are boats on the lake, and you can swim too. There's a bridge over the lake. This is one of the largest parks in London. I'd like to go to … because … *Individuelle S-Antworten*

Dialogues: Useful questions and phrases

• You went to … last year. Did you like it? • How was your visit to … last year? • What did you do/see there? • What did you like the best? • Was there something you didn't like about it? • Did it cost a lot to go there? • What advice can you give me for my visit?	• Yes, I had fun/a good time there! • One of the best things about my visit was … • I did lots of/I saw interesting things like … • It was OK, but … • I really liked …, but … • You need/don't need lots of money to … • Before you go/when you're there, remember to …

Dialogues: Model answer

A: You went to Covent Garden last year. Did you like it?
B: Yes, my family and I did. It was great!
A: What did you do?
B: Well, first I went to the shops because I wanted to buy souvenirs. But I didn't have much money, so I couldn't buy lots.
A: So was everything expensive?
B: No! We watched some great street shows, and they were free!
A: What else did you see there?
B: We saw people from many different countries. It was an interesting crowd!
A: What advice can you give me for my visit?
B: Watch as many street shows as you can. They're great!

▲ **Role play:** Someone steals your money and your partner's money when you're waiting at a Tube station! What are you going to do? Act the scene.

Green Line 2
Vorschläge zur Leistungsmessung
ISBN 978-3-12-834224-5

Unit 4

Warm up: • Which sports do you like/not like? Why/why not?
• Have you ever had a funny/exciting/embarrassing experience while you did a sport? Describe it.

Monologues: Model answers

1. In this picture there are two football teams (girls). The game has just ended. The team in black and white has just won the game 3:2, and the team members are cheering. Lots of people in the crowd are cheering too. The team in yellow and blue has lost, and they're sad. Some of the people in the crowd are sad too.

2. In this picture there are two football teams (boys). The score is 4:3 but the game isn't over yet. It has stopped because Sam Smith has hurt his leg. The player in the white shirt with number 11 looks very worried. He probably caused the injury. The other players and the crowd look upset too. They don't know if the game can go on.

3. In this picture, Lisa Winter has just won the mini marathon, and she looks very happy! She's cheering! Runner 106 is second, and he's disappointed. This is a race where boys and girls run together. A lot of other runners aren't very far behind her, and they are still doing their best to run as fast as they can.

4. In this picture, two clowns are running in the mini marathon. Suddenly they stop because they want to take a selfie. Then there is an accident and John Brown falls because of them. He can't get up because he has hurt his ankle. The clowns look upset. The fans and the other runners look horrified.

Dialogues: Useful questions and phrases

• That's great you/your team won the game/mini marathon! How did you feel?
• You were hurt but your team still won. How was that possible?
• Why do you think your team won the game?
• Was the race/game a challenge for you?
• What did you do to prepare for the race?

• I'm sorry that the game/mini marathon didn't go well for you. What happened?
• How are you? Can you already play/run again?
• What did the boy who hurt you say/do?
• How did you feel when you fell?
• What have you learned from this race/game?

Dialogues: Model answers

1.
A: Hello Sally! That's great that you won the mini marathon! How did you feel then?
B: At first I couldn't believe it. But then I was so happy and excited! I cheered and cheered!
A: What did you do to prepare for the race?
B: I did what I always do. I ran for an hour at least three times a week, and I got lots of sleep and ate healthy food. That's my secret.
A: Was the race a challenge for you?
B: Yes, it was! Some of the other runners were very fast, so it wasn't easy to stay in front!
A: Are you looking forward to your next race?
B: Yes, I am! It's going to be a good one!
A: Thanks for the interview!

2.
A: Hello Sam! How's your ankle?
B: It's a lot better, thanks.
A: What a dramatic game! After you were hurt, your team still won! How was that possible?
B: The boy who played for me was really great.
A: Did the other player say he was sorry?
B: Yes, of course. He still feels bad, but accidents happen in sports.
A: How did you feel when it happened?
B: I was surprised, and my ankle really hurt!
A: What have you learned from this game?
B: I've learned that I shouldn't get upset when accidents happen!

 Role play: Partner A is a player from the losing team in picture 1. Partner B is a member of the winning team. Partner A thinks it isn't fair that the other team won and talks to Partner B about it. What do they say to each other?

Green Line 2
Vorschläge zur Leistungsmessung
ISBN 978-3-12-834224-5

Unit 5

Warm up: • Which kinds of media are the most important for you? Give reasons.
• Have you had an interesting/exciting/embarrassing/funny experience on a social network? Describe it.

Monologues: Model answers

1. In this picture, a girl has brought a mobile/smartphone to class, but she isn't allowed to. The teacher is angry and she wants the girl to give it to her. The girl looks embarrassed/upset. Some of the other children are laughing and whispering.	**2.** In this picture, a boy is playing video games. He looks like he's played for a long time and he doesn't want to do anything else. He hasn't tidied his room or tried to do well in school (his test on his desk isn't good). His friend wants to talk to him, but he isn't listening.
3. In this picture, one girl has gotten a bad message/text on her mobile/smartphone and is showing it to her friend. Her friend looks like it's a shock for her also. She has her arm around her friend because her friend feels very bad. She's trying to help her friend.	**4.** In this picture, a boy is online/taking part in a forum and he's chatting with someone (CoolKid3). CoolKid 3 wants to know where the boy lives, but the boy looks nervous. He's not sure if he should tell him. He's started to write something, but he's not sure if/how he should go on.

Dialogues: Useful questions and phrases

• What should I do? • Have you got any ideas? • Can you please help me? • You're upset, aren't you? Can I help you?	• Why don't you … • You should/shouldn't… • You could … • Have you tried …

Dialogues: Model answers

1. A: Karen, you know you aren't allowed to have that in class. Give it to me, please! B: But Ms Waters, my mum … A: I don't want a discussion! B: But my mum is in hospital! It's an emergency (*Notfall*)! My dad wants to call me … A: Oh dear, I'm so sorry! B: Well, is it OK if …	**2.** A: Hey Nick, what about a game of football? B: Uh, not now. I have to finish this game. A: But you've said that for a week! Come on! B: Not now. I need to get 100 more points … A: Hey, you don't look good! Your face is white! Why don't you come outside! You'll feel better! B: I don't want to play football! Just go! A: I'm worried about you! You should …
3. A: Here! Read what Sarah's written about me! I can't believe she can be so nasty! B: That's awful! Why did she write this? A: I guess because I didn't invite her to my last party. But she didn't invite me to hers! B: That's no reason to write such bad things! A: What should I do? I'm so angry! B: Well, why don't we …	**4.** A: Hi Peter, it's me. CoolKid3 has written to me again. Now he wants my address … B: You mean where you live? A: Yeah! Should I tell him? B: No! You don't know who this person really is! Maybe he's crazy! Don't talk to him again! And I think you should tell your parents! A: Well OK, but could you please …

 Discussion: Some people get upset about the things they read or see on social networks. Talk with your partner about the things you think shouldn't be online and why, and discuss what you can do about it if you find them there.

Green Line 2
Vorschläge zur Leistungsmessung
ISBN 978-3-12-834224-5

Unit 6

Warm up: • Describe an interesting or a funny or a scary experience you had while you were travelling.
 • Have you (or someone you know well) had to move house? How was it for you/him/her?

Monologues: Model answers

1. In this picture, a family discovers that someone has been in their hotel room when they were out. Their things are all over the room. The person who was there probably stole something. Everyone is very upset. The boy is calling the receptionist to tell her what happened. She's upset too.

2. In this picture, a father and a girl are in a tour bus which is leaving, but the mother is still waiting in the queue for the toilet. The door is closed, so she doesn't hear that the bus is leaving. The father is trying to call her, and the girl is trying to get the bus driver's attention. She's hitting the wall behind him.

3. In this picture, a boy has hurt his leg when he and his class were on a hiking trip. Someone had to call the emergency service, and now they are helping him. He's talking to someone on his mobile about what happened. The other students and the teacher look upset/sad.

4. In this picture, a girl must move house and she's sad about it. Her friends aren't happy, but they're trying to help her so she doesn't feel so sad. They've given her present (the book). Someone is taking boxes of her things out of her room. There isn't much still in her room.

Dialogues: Model answers

1.
A: Hello, is this the reception desk? Someone has been in our room and stolen our things!
B: What? Are you sure?
A: Of course! A lot of money is missing and my mother's jewellery too!
B: This is horrible! I'm going to call the police right now! Then I'll come to your room to help you. Then we'll …

2.
A: Oh no! We're leaving the/café/restaurant!
B: What? Where's Mum?
A: She's still waiting in the queue for the toilet!
B: And she doesn't hear her mobile!
A: And she doesn't hear that we're leaving!
B: We must try to get the bus driver's attention! Let's …

3.
A: Hey Mum! Something has happened. I hurt my leg on the hiking trip.
B: Oh no! Is it bad? What does the doctor say?
A: Well I think my leg is broken. I must go to hospital. Everyone's upset.
B: Oh dear, which hospital? I'll come right now!
A: Wait a minute. I'll ask …

4.
A: Wendy, we're sorry you have to move too, but we'll come and visit you!
B: I don't want to leave you two! I'm so sad!
A: So are we, but maybe when you read this you'll get excited about London!
B: Thanks! Let's plan your visit and I'll feel better!
A: When we visit I'd like to …

 Discussion: You and your partner should each finish the sentence "If you want to do something good for others, you should …" Then compare your answers. How are your ideas similar or different? What do you think about each other's ideas? Discuss.

Bewertung der Sprachkompetenz (Units 1 to 6)
Auf der letzten Seite befindet sich ein Bewertungsbogen, mit dem Lehrer(innen) die Sprachkompetenz der Schüler evaluieren können. Der Bewertungsbogen ist auch in editierbarer Form auf der beiliegenden CD-ROM enthalten.

Green Line 2
Vorschläge zur Leistungsmessung
ISBN 978-3-12-834224-5

Bewertungsbogen

Bewertung der Sprachkompetenz	voll	nahezu	im Wesentlichen	teilweise	kaum	nicht
Kriterien / deren Erfüllung						
inhaltlich richtig						
inhaltlich vollständig/ ausführlich						
sprachlich verständlich						
sprachlich korrekt						
phonetisch korrekt						
intonatorisch korrekt						
adressaten-/ situationsgerecht						
selbstständig						

Green Line 2
Vorschläge zur Leistungsmessung
ISBN 978-3-12-834224-5

Inhalt der Audio-CD

Hörverstehenstexte

Track	Unit	Test	Page	Title	Time
1	1	1	5	How were your holidays?	01:48
2	1	2	6	Trouble on Red Nose Day	01:27
3	2	1	15	The Sign Language Club	01:31
4	2	2	16	Using a timetable	02:08
5	3	1	25	Holiday plans	01:36
6	3	2	26	A tour of London	02:48
7	4	1	36	What's important	01:25
8	4	2	37	A dramatic sea rescue	01:32
9	5	1	46	Talking about advice	01:26
10	5	2	47	A school project	01:18
11	6	1	56	A family trip	01:51
12	6	2	57	The Newcastle Morning Show	01:41

Gesamtspielzeit: 20:39

Inhalt der CD-ROM

Filmsequenzen

Unit	Test	Page	Title	Time
3	17 Viewing	35	A look at the Thames	02:26
64	17 Viewing	67	A look at Cornwall	01:43

Gesamtspielzeit: 03:69

Außerdem finden Sie auf dieser CD-ROM:
- Materialien für Klassenarbeiten (inkl. Materialien für Viewing-Tests) und Lösungen
- alle *Speaking cards* und die dazugehörenden *Teacher's notes*
- alle Transkripte zu den Hörverstehenstexten und Filmsequenzen
- Förderempfehlungsmaterialien
- ein Bewertungsraster für die Speaking-Tests
- alle Hörverstehenstexte im mp3-Format

Systemvoraussetzungen der CD-ROM
- Webbrowser ab:
  Microsoft Internet Explorer 5.5, Mozilla Firefox 2.0, Safari 3.0, Opera 9.0, Konqueror 3.2
- PC: Pentium 166 MHz
- Mac: 400 Mhz, G3 PowerPC oder Intel-basierter Macintosh Computer
- 512 MB RAM
- CD-ROM Laufwerk
- Adobe Reader ab Version 5
- Adobe Flash Player ab Version 9
- Medienplayer für mp3-Dateien
- Microsoft Office oder kompatible Textverarbeitung.

Sollten Sie Probleme mit dem vorliegenden Programm haben, finden Sie in der Datei „Hotline.txt",
die sich auf der obersten Ebene der CD-ROM befindet, unsere Kontaktdaten und weitere Hilfestellungen.

Auf der CD-ROM befindet sich ein ausführliches Handbuch zum Programm.